Wakefield Press

South Australia on the Eve of War

South Australia on the Eve of War

Edited by
MELANIE OPPENHEIMER, MARGARET ANDERSON AND MANDY PAUL

Wakefield Press
16 Rose Street
Mile End
South Australia 5031
www.wakefieldpress.com.au

First published 2017

Cover designed by Liz Nicholson, designBITE
Cover illustration: Crowds gathered outside government offices, Victoria Square, Adelaide, following the announcement of war, 5 August 1914. [History SA, SAGPC GN 01360]
Edited by Emily Hart, Wakefield Press
Typeset by Michael Deves, Wakefield Press

National Library of Australia Cataloguing-in-Publication entry

Title:	South Australia on the eve of war / edited by Melanie Oppenheimer, Margaret Anderson and Mandy Paul.
ISBN:	978 1 74305 474 1 (paperback).
Subjects:	World War, 1914–1918 – South Australia. South Australia – Politics and government – 1901–1914. South Australia – Social conditions – 1901–1914. South Australia – Economic conditions – 1901–1914.
Other Creators/ Contributors:	Oppenheimer, Melanie, editor. Anderson, Margaret, editor. Paul, Mandy, editor.

For

Jill Roe and John Bannon

two giants of Australian history

Contents

Acknowledgements

South Australia on the Eve of War was a two-day symposium organised by History SA, in association with Flinders University, the University of Adelaide, the Professional Historians Association and the University of South Australia. It was held at the campus of the University of Adelaide on the first weekend of August 2014 to mark the centenary of the beginning of the First World War.

Selected papers from the symposium have been gathered in this publication. The editors would like to acknowledge the assistance received from a range of people in bringing this project to fruition. Thanks are due to Professor John Williams for his assistance with editing his late friend and colleague Dr John Bannon's chapter. The late Emerita Professor Jill Roe agreed to write a short chapter on the Eyre Peninsula and Dr Stephanie James assisted with the research and final preparation of this chapter.

A number of people have helped the editors turn a collection of papers into a manuscript; our thanks are due to Dr Margrette Kleinig and Dr Carolyn Collins, and to Suzanne Redman for image production.

We would also like to thank Michael Bollen and the team at Wakefield Press for their support with this project. South Australian history would be all the poorer without the presence of a publisher such as Wakefield Press that recognises the integral importance of local- and state-focused histories and champions it on a national and international stage.

This publication is supported by a History SA publication grant.

1

Progressive conservatism and boundless optimism
South Australia on the eve of war

MELANIE OPPENHEIMER AND MARGRETTE KLEINIG

South Australia entered the war in August 1914 in a similar fashion to the other Australian states. Enthusiastic crowds of upwards of 20,000 people crammed into Elder Park, a large open space nestled between the city centre and the Torrens River and dominated by a Victorian rotunda. They greeted the news with cheers and bravado much like for a football or cricket game. The newspapers had been full of reports leading up to the announcement of war on 5 August, and in months to come the pent-up anticipation led to public displays of loyalty to King and Country across the state. Following the tradition of past conflicts, patriotic funds to assist the war effort were formed, including the South Australian division of the British Red Cross Society, led by the Governor's wife, Lady Galway. A citizen army quickly took shape as thousands of men answered the call to volunteer for active service. Many had undergone compulsory military training as part of the 1911 Commonwealth Government's Universal Service Scheme.

This is a story we know reasonably well, and the centenary of World War I has reminded us once more of the sacrifices made by the generations that experienced that 'war to end all wars'. But what was South Australia like in the years leading up to

August 1914? What kind of society was it, what was it like to live there, and what were the major issues of the period in South Australia, the third largest state of the new Commonwealth at the time with the third biggest capital city, Adelaide? Following on from eminent historians such as Peter Howell, Eric Richards, and others who have explored this period in South Australian history, this book seeks to answer some of these questions. It is based on a symposium held in Adelaide in 2014 that brought together historians with an interest in these questions to explore a number of themes relevant to South Australia on the eve of war. This chapter aims to provide a snapshot of the state as well as some context and background. It is not intended to be comprehensive, but instead to offer an overview of the more detailed analysis that is delivered by the chapters that follow.

Three individuals – David Unaipon, Catherine Helen Spence and Douglas Mawson – encapsulate the spirit of South Australia in the years between Federation in 1901 and the eve of war. All, too, have graced our paper currency at one point or another, an indication of their national importance. Catherine Helen Spence, who died in Adelaide in 1910, was described as 'the leading woman in public affairs at the turn of the century in Australia': South Australia's Chief Justice further described her as 'the most distinguished woman they had had in Australia'.[1] At the forefront of the first-wave feminist movement, which included ensuring South Australia was the first Australian state to secure voting rights for women in 1894, Spence became Australia's first female political candidate, standing unsuccessfully for election as a delegate to the 1897 Australasian Federal Convention.[2]

'Preacher, author and inventor' David Unaipon was once described as the 'best-known Aborigine in the Commonwealth' in the early twentieth century.[3] Born in 1872 at the Point

McLeay Mission (now Raukkan) on the edge of the River Murray Lower Lakes, Unaipon was, on the eve of war, in his early forties. Interested in 'philosophy, science and music' and in recording his people's oral stories and traditions, Unaipon had 'led a deputation urging government control of Point McLeay Mission' in 1912, and the following year gave evidence to a state government Royal Commission into Aboriginal matters.[4]

In early 1914 Douglas Mawson triumphantly returned from the Antarctic, where he had led Australia's 'first scientific exploring endeavour beyond the Australian continent'.[5] Lecturer in mineralogy and petrology at the University of Adelaide, Mawson was physicist on the Shackleton expedition (1907–1909) that aimed to reach the South Geographic Pole. While leading the Australasian Antarctic Expedition of 1911–1914, he made scientific advances in 'cartography, geology, meteorology, aurora, geomagnetism, biology and marine science'.[6]

These three remarkable people, who pushed the boundaries in their own particular spheres in unexpected and very different ways, point to important social, political and cultural developments in late nineteenth- and early twentieth-century South Australia that had an impact both nationally and internationally. The long-running economic recession of the later nineteenth century lingered into the early years of the new century but was then followed by a decade of relative prosperity in South Australia. The return of economic confidence from about 1905 brought political pressure upon successive governments to open further rural land to agricultural development, to modernise public infrastructure and utilities, and to implement major public works. Land was widely cleared and ongoing settlement established, especially on the Eyre Peninsula and in the Murray Mallee.[7] Fruit blocks were introduced in the Riverland, heralding the future development of an industry important to the South Australian economy. Nonetheless a severe drought in 1914 was a sobering check upon rampant expansion.

The first federal census of 1911 recorded South Australia's population as 408,558 persons – nine per cent of the Australian population. The figure was exclusive of Aboriginal people, who were not counted in the census.[8] However, 'between initial European Colonization and Federation in 1901', the population of Aboriginal people in South Australia is considered to have been reduced by 50 per cent from an estimated original population of 10,000–15,000.[9] The balance between the sexes in the European population was relatively even, with 103 males per 100 females in 1911. Only Victoria had a more even ratio, with 99 per 100 men to women. More people lived in regional towns and rural areas than in Adelaide city and its suburbs, although the proportions were beginning to shift. The overwhelming majority of the population (86 per cent) was Australian born. Of those born overseas, most were from the United Kingdom (11 per cent), with a further two per cent born in Continental Europe, mostly in Germany and Scandinavia.[10] Until World War I the German-born and their descendants are estimated to have comprised about 10 per cent of South Australia's population.[11] Engaged in all aspects of South Australian community life, they were proportionately the largest of the immigrant national groups with the exception of those from the British Isles.

South Australia had vibrant social and community structures, not least in its capital city, Adelaide, termed 'the city of churches'. Whether this term is a valid one is open to question for more people went to church in Victoria than in South Australia; as Peter Howell has pointed out, in 1901 there were 'four times as

'First successful aeroplane flight over Adelaide (A.W. Jones, pilot), 2 January 1914'. On the left is the Institute Building, corner of North Terrace and Kintore Avenue; the dome further along North Terrace is of the Exhibition Building. [Photographer: Henry Krischock. SLSA B 285]

many pubs' as churches in Adelaide city.[12] But perhaps South Australians were more cautious and frugal. Between 1902 and 1907 the state had the highest rate of saving in the nation. It was also safer to walk the streets. The chances of being a victim of a major criminal offence were considered to be less than half the national average.[13] In terms of social activities, the first South Australian theatre designed and erected expressly as a 'picture palace', the Pavilion, opened in Rundle Street in 1912, with over half a million admission tickets sold in the first year. A second, Wondergraph, opened in Hindley Street the following year.[14] By 1914 Adelaide had a thriving vaudeville, concert and theatre scene for general amusements. Patrons could attend a live show at Theatre Royal, the New Tivoli Theatre and the King's Theatre, or take in a show at the Hippodrome or Empire Theatre Pictures. As in all Australian states, sport was a much-loved recreational activity, with horse racing, cricket, lacrosse, lawn tennis, boxing and Australian Rules Football very popular across the state. The remodelled South Australian Football League was formed in 1907, and three years later, at an Interstate Football Carnival held in Adelaide, numbers on guernseys were allocated to players for the first time.[15]

The years before the First World War were a dynamic period in the state legislature, as they were at a Commonwealth level. Arbitration legislation and wages boards were implemented and government welfare provisions initiated. In 1912 a state Industrial Court was established in South Australia.[16] The Harvester (Federal) Judgement of 1907, which introduced the concept of an arbitrated 'living wage' to enable a (male) breadwinner to support himself and his dependants, set the scene for future determinations regarding minimum wages and conditions for Australian workers.[17] However, as Margaret Anderson suggests in her chapter in this volume, this had negative implications for women workers. South Australians also benefited from important social welfare provisions introduced by the Commonwealth Government in the five years before the First World War. Age and invalid pensions were introduced in 1909 and 1910. Means-tested and with age, residence and 'character' qualifications, the pensions were designed to assist those most in need – that is, those without an income and lacking the ability to work.[18] Moreover, in 1912 a maternity allowance (the first form of family allowance) was introduced by the federal government. It was a non-means-tested lump sum cash payment to a mother on the birth of a child. However, Aboriginal mothers and women defined as 'non-citizens' were ineligible.[19]

The first Wages Board was established at the turn of the century to regulate the wages of women and girls after a select committee had examined the 'alleged sweating evil'.[20] Sweated labour, especially in clothing factories and in 'outwork', in regard to both men and women but especially of concern in relation to women in the clothing industry, had been a social and political issue for more than two decades. There had been slowly widening occupational opportunities within the public service for women, especially in teaching, nursing and the clerical sector. More than a third of employed women (36.2 per cent) worked in domestic service (both private and institutional) despite a fall of almost 10 per cent in this sector between the 1901 and 1911 censuses. The participation rates in the manufacturing (32.5 per cent), commercial (15.6 per cent) and professional (13.5 per cent) sectors, which constituted the remaining bulk of the female workforce, each rose between the 1901 and 1911 censuses. Nonetheless, in the half century between 1871 and 1921, the annual growth of the female workforce in Adelaide was at its lowest (1.2 per cent) between the 1901 and 1911 censuses – as it was in Melbourne – perhaps an indication, as W.A. Sinclair suggests, that families were weighing up the contribution which women, especially daughters, could make to the household economy through services rather than income.[21]

The greatest number of males engaged in the workforce was in primary production, especially in agriculture, with manufacturing and building in the industrial sector forming the next largest group. Commercial employment followed some distance behind in third place.[22] Although South Australian workers are considered to have 'usually been less militant than their interstate counterparts', the state experienced its worst period of industrial strife for two decades in 1910 and

1911.[23] Confrontation occurred over falling real wages as well as conditions such as demand for shorter hours of work. In 1914 the average weekly hours of work prescribed by the state industrial awards was 'just over 48 hours for males and 49 hours for females'.[24]

As suggested by Susan Magarey and others, the period was an optimistic one for many women.[25] Suffrage in South Australia had been achieved twenty years earlier and women's social reformist organisations were very active, especially among the middle classes. One of the most important was the Women's Non-Party Political Association, formed in 1909. The Association, later known as the League of Women Voters of South Australia, was an influential lobby group in the political sphere. The Association's aim was social change through education, especially in practical matters affecting women, children and the home. Its platform included 'equal federal marriage and divorce laws', 'equal rights over children', 'equal pay for equal work' and the appointment of female Justices of the Peace (an aim achieved with the first appointments in 1915 by the Vaughan government).[26] Enabling legislation in 1911 also meant that women could practise the profession of law.[27]

In January 1911, after administering the Northern Territory for almost 50 years, South Australia ceded the Territory to the Commonwealth Government.[28] The following year the Verran government, the first majority Labor government in Australia (and in the world), set a general election in train by engineering a crisis over the constitutional relationship between the two Houses of Parliament, basically over control of the Legislative Council (or Upper House).[29] The 'brief and spirited election campaign' of 1912, which followed the industrial unrest mentioned earlier, and in which Labor suffered a major defeat, was 'described at the time as the most important and fiercest political battle ever fought in South Australia'.[30] The campaign elicited much interest, with a considerable number of persons reportedly adding their names to the voting lists for both the Legislative Council and House of Assembly: almost 14,000 to the former and more than 41,000 to the latter.[31]

Modernity in transport had become a political issue. In 1913 there were over a quarter of a million horses in South Australia, but their pre-eminent position in regard to transport was about to be lost.[32] The first electric tram was seen in Adelaide streets in 1909, after the government had earlier created the Municipal Tramways Trust and purchased the tram system from private companies.[33] South Australia was the first state to require

'The end of one era and the beginning of another'. On the right a horse tram, on the left a new electric tram. North Terrace, looking east from Frome Road, 1909. [SLSA B 4364]

Camel Team used in the construction of the East–West Railway, Port Augusta to Kalgoorlie, 1914. [SLSA B 240]

vehicle registration and to issue driving licences (1907), but did not institute skill testing. There were fewer than 1000 cars on the roads in 1910, but more than 1500 motorcycles.[34]

A new program of railway construction was implemented. Lines linked the new farming lands and mining areas within South Australia to ports, and a line was laid between Mount Gambier and Portland in Victoria.[35] In early negotiations regarding the transfer of the administration of the Northern Territory to the Commonwealth, South Australian Premier Tom Price expected that the federal government would build a north-south transcontinental railway linking Oodnadatta and Palmerston (now Darwin), an expectation which was not fulfilled for another 100 years.[36] However, the construction of a railway line between Port Augusta and Kalgoorlie, commenced in 1912, facilitated the linking of Perth with Sydney and the establishment of a train service which is now known simply as the Indian Pacific.

In September 1914, after more than a decade of negotiation, the River Murray Waters Agreement was secured by Premier Peake with the governments of New South Wales, Victoria and the Commonwealth for the 'building of a series of locks, to store water for irrigation' and to facilitate navigation'.[37] Less successful was the long negotiation (over four decades) and the resulting High Court Challenge by South Australia in 1911 over the state's eastern land boundary with Victoria. A surveying mistake located the boundary a few kilometres east of the position specified in imperial instruments, resulting, as Peter Howell has outlined, 'in the loss of 1,300 square kilometres of South Australian land, much of it suitable for agriculture, grazing or irrigation'.[38]

The major sources of wealth in the state were beginning to expand beyond the primary production sector and into mercantile, manufacturing and financial activity. Family companies that later became household names were prominent in this period through both national and international markets. G.H. Michell processed wool and hides, Seppelt & Sons and the Reynell family produced award-winning wine and, on the eve of war, Henry and Edward Holden extended their business to include the manufacture of the burgeoning trade in motorcycle sidecars and painted car bodies.[39] A. Simpson & Son, later producers of whitegoods, were the first in Australia to manufacture enamelware. A.A. Simpson, a director of the company, was Lord Mayor of Adelaide in this period and, with his wife, was very prominent in patriotic endeavours during the war.[40]

In response to the return of prosperity and initiatives for agricultural development, major public works construction and the small, developing manufacturing sector, the government bowed to pressure for additional labour for these industries and reintroduced publicly funded immigration. With the exception of Tasmania, the other Australian states had re-established or expanded their immigration schemes several years earlier, but memories of the acute recession and labour unrest of the late nineteenth century had caused successive South Australian governments to exercise caution and delay the reintroduction of publicly funded immigration until 1911.[41] The Commonwealth's Immigration Restriction Act of 1901 (known as the White Australia Policy) had little direct influence on South Australia's assisted immigration program since the state continued to focus its recruitment program upon the British Isles, as it had done in the nineteenth century.[42] As part of the response to the demand for labour in agriculture, the government implemented a new initiative, the British farm apprenticeship scheme, for farmers in rural areas to train (under formal agreement) young male immigrants aged between 15 and 19 years.[43] It was additionally stated that local sources could not meet the demand for female domestic assistance in private households; the health of mothers and their children, and hence future prosperity, were said to be at risk without additional help within the home. A contraction in the domestic service sector of the employed workforce during the first decade of the new century, combined with a rise in South Australia's birthrate, was successfully used by employers to apply political pressure to include this class of labour within the government's immigration program.[44] With government assistance, more than 7000 immigrants arrived in South Australia before the program was curtailed by the war.

The following nine chapters in this book take as their focus a range of themes and subject matter relevant to South Australia on the eve of war. We are honoured to be able to publish work by the late John Bannon in Chapter Two. It explores the political dimensions of the transformation of South Australia from a colony to a state within the Commonwealth of Australia and sets the scene for the chapters that follow. South Australia was always very supportive of the national project but like the other states, found the adjustment difficult especially at the imperial level. Despite playing a leading role, Bannon explains that South Australia was also disappointed at its lack of influence at the national level in the years after 1901.

Chapter Three, authored by Margaret Anderson and Alison Mackinnon, focuses on the lives of women and their families. They suggest that although there were significant developments for women, both inside and outside of marriage, in the period to 1914, there was also much continuity in their day-to-day lives based around the family. Despite technological developments in the domestic sphere such as the gas stove and modifications in women's dress codes, it depended on where you lived and your status as to how much these impacted on women and the modern family.

In Chapter Four, Mandy Paul takes as her subject the Aboriginal people of South Australia and their relationship to the state in the years between Federation and the outbreak of war. She explains that Aboriginal people were viewed as three separate groups: those in the so-called 'settled districts', those living in Central Australia and the far north of South Australia, and thirdly those living in the remote tropical north. During this period, legislation was enacted at the state level that was to control rather than protect Aboriginal people, which had ramifications for decades to come. The Aborigines Act of 1911 led to segregation from the wider community and overarching powers for the Chief Protector of Aborigines. Royal Commissions in 1913 and 1914, too, saw those defined as 'half castes' coming under the control of the state. Yet despite this, Paul reminds us that a significant number of Aboriginal men enlisted in the army during the First World War, something we are still learning about today.

Chapters Five and Six shift our focus to rural South Australia on the eve of war. Elspeth Grant examines the farm apprenticeship scheme for British boys aged between 15 to 19 years, which revolved around supporting an expansion of the South Australian agriculture project in the first decades of the twentieth century and brings together concepts of migration and imperialism. Timing is crucial here, with the first group of farm apprentices only arriving in June 1913, and 171 boys in total arriving on three-year secondments until the scheme was suspended on the outbreak of war. A significant number of these young men – more than three quarters, Grant tells us – later enlisted in the Australian Imperial Force. Well-known Australian historian Jill Roe takes a personal look at the Eyre Peninsula, where she was born and raised, to provide an important rural perspective. Through an analysis of local newspapers, Roe demonstrates that rural people were well aware of the storm brewing in Europe and its possible consequences, and that although there was initial support for the war, enthusiasm did not last.

Anyone who visits Adelaide for the first time cannot help but notice the distinctive bluestone buildings, symmetrical streetscapes, ordered public gardens and open spaces – Mark Twain was smitten, as many others continue to be. In Chapter

Seven, Christine Garnaut examines the physical planning and development of Adelaide from its beginnings in the 1830s through to 1914. She gives us a wonderful insight into this renowned 'Garden City of the South', a capital city that was a close third behind Sydney and Melbourne for its population size, physical grandeur and national importance on the outbreak of war.

The next three chapters focus on minority groups and how they positioned themselves as part of the South Australian project in the lead up to World War I. In Chapter Eight, Margaret Allen confronts the impact of the Immigration Restriction Act of 1901 – one of the first pieces of legislation of the new Commonwealth – on the small, and hitherto little-known, Indian community of South Australia. She explores their experiences, especially that of merchant Bhagat Singh, and how he and others built connections with other groups, such as the Chinese community, similarly affected by the White Australia Policy. Peter Monteath takes the more well-known German community of South Australia as his subject matter in Chapter Nine, and asks why, after decades of co-existing in peaceful harmony together with the British majority, the relationship between the two national groups deteriorated so quickly on the outbreak of war. His perspective is that dominant Australian nationalism, fuelled by Federation rhetoric that was laced with racism and a fervent 'Anglo' ideology, helped to tear German South Australians apart on the outbreak of war. Yet, as Monteath suggests, the German community never felt more connected to South Australia than in 1914. Stephanie James continues the theme of minority responses in our final chapter, looking at the Irish in South Australia. South Australia's Irish population was lower than that of the eastern states at just under 15 per cent. Using the Home Rule Bill debates from Britain as the basis of her study, James argues that Catholicism and Irish immigrants were always divisive issues in South Australia, never more so than on the outbreak of war. Despite unconditional Irish–South Australian imperial loyalty in 1914, the same could not be said for how they were accepted by the majority of South Australians.

On 5 August 1914, when South Australians went to war, they had no idea of what was to come. Those who went to listen to world famous pianist Harold Bauer, on his final night at the Adelaide Town Hall, play his programme laced with Beethoven minuets and sonatas and Schumann's 'Scenes from Childhood' had little understanding of how their worlds were about to change irrevocably.[45] This book aims to provide readers with insights into what kind of place South Australia was in 1914 and how that helps us to understand the responses to a war that consumed the state and its people for the next four years.

2

Adjustment to statehood
South Australia from the Boer War to the Great War

JOHN BANNON[1]

On 1 January 1901, sixty-five years after its foundation, South Australia was transformed from a self-governing colony of the British Empire to a member state of the Commonwealth of Australia. There were high expectations that this would solve a number of long-term economic problems, providing advantages to the central state that would lead to prosperity and security. The South Australian delegations to the Australasian Federal Conventions of 1891 and 1897–1898 were praised and respected for their ability and cohesion. They had managed to get many of their aims written into the Australian Constitution and had a major impact on the document that was finally adopted.[2] The South Australian electors had voted solidly for it in two referendums. They had every reason to expect that benefits would flow.

Now, almost fourteen years on – August 1914 – the Commonwealth, as part of the British Empire, was at war. How was South Australia placed as a member of the Commonwealth? How had its political progress been affected by its new role as a state rather than a province? What was the state of its economy and what contribution should it be expected to make to the war effort? On the eve of war these questions demanded attention.

Federal expectations: the balance sheet

All the states, and particularly South Australia, found it hard to adjust to their new status at the imperial level. This was despite their continued right to recommend to the monarch the appointment of governors and, through them, maintain direct links to the Crown in Britain. The premiers had successfully opposed an early Commonwealth attempt to make all communications go through the Governor-General, following a Canadian model. Each state still maintained quasi-diplomatic and trade representation through their agents-general. But the moment of truth had come with the convening of the 1907 Imperial Conference, when the leaders of the British Empire were called to London for a major negotiation on the future relations of the Empire following the Boer War and South African unification. The premiers of Australia were not invited. South Australia's Tom Price led a spirited campaign to the British Government in 1906, arguing that the 'Prime Ministers of the Australian States should be summoned to the Imperial Conference'. In a long and detailed petition, he argued that the Constitution made it clear that the states were 'independent of the federal government and in no way subordinate to it'.[3] Despite the powers granted to the Commonwealth, he claimed that 'by far the larger and more important work of the government of Australia remains and must continue to remain with the States'. The fact that what we would now call 'foreign affairs' was not seen then as a prerogative of the Commonwealth but remained an imperial responsibility gave some more strength to the claim.

The imperial government refrained from a decision. Price's petition was referred to the Commonwealth for advice and comment, which naturally objected strongly, and so it got nowhere. Clearly 'Australia' in the imperial and international environment was embodied in the Commonwealth government, and the states had no role to play there. Domestic federal issues were now their only concern. A stocktake of the impact of Federation on South Australia on the eve of war provided a very mixed report.

Governance

South Australians had pioneered the female franchise. South Australian women were the only women in Australia to take part in the election for delegates to the Convention of 1897–1898 and the subsequent referendums that led to the Commonwealth Bill.[4] This was a major factor in the Commonwealth adopting female franchise in its Electoral Act, although the right had still not been extended in some states such as Victoria, where it was not granted until 1908. Although not successful in giving franchise to Aboriginal people, South Australians had argued successfully for maintenance of the right to vote of those who already held the entitlement at state level.

The delegation had stressed the role of the Senate as a states' house to protect the interests of the smaller states. But after the first Senate it had become increasingly a creature of party rather than state, with big majorities for one or other party ensuring that its independent status was not preserved despite the powers it enjoyed under the Constitution.

There was an expectation, heightened by the prominence and ability of its delegates at the Convention, that the South Australians would have a major influence in the executive of the Commonwealth. As was to be expected, eight of South Australia's twelve delegates at the 1891 and 1897 conventions successfully stood for the first Federal Parliament in 1901. They were joined by other prominent South Australian political figures. Seven of them were ministers at some point over the next fifteen years in different administrations, but none achieved the office of prime minister or leader of the opposition. Charles Kingston's illness at a critical time robbed him of any chance of being prime minister in 1904, and his term in the first Cabinet was brief. Egerton Batchelor, destined for great things in the Labor ascendancy under Fisher, died suddenly and prematurely in 1911. A disillusioned Sir John Downer did not stand for a second term and returned to state politics. Two of the ablest delegates, Frederick Holder and Richard Baker, became inaugural Speaker and President of the Senate respectively. The promise of major influence was not fulfilled.

Legal recognition

Constitutional provisions establishing the High Court and giving it the role as the 'umpire' of disputes between the Commonwealth and the states over their respective powers was critical to the working of the Federation. From the appointment of the first three justices in 1903, all of whom had been Convention delegates and key draftsmen of the Constitution, it largely kept the federal pact. Despite some decisions that seemed to favour an increase in central power at the expense of the states, the judges, even after being joined by two more in 1906 who had been delegates with more centralised views, still broadly interpreted the Constitution as protecting the rights of all its members.

The disappointment was that by 1914 no South Australian had become a justice of the High Court that Symon (as Chair of the Judicial Committee), Downer and others had been so instrumental in creating. The initial decision to confine the numbers on the Bench to three rather than the five envisaged, the dominance of the Sydney and Melbourne bars, and the ego of South Australian Chief Justice Samuel Way all worked to frustrate the legitimate expectations that South Australia would be represented. The prime early candidate, Sir John Downer, was twice overlooked: firstly, when Prime Minister Edmund Barton decided that he would retire from politics and take one of the three initial positions himself; and secondly, when Prime Minister Alfred Deakin's antipathy to Downer saw him offer the job to Sir Samuel Way. Way refused, believing that his status as a member of the Privy Council was superior to that of High Court Justice, and that the High Court would not become a real force in the Australian judicial system, so Deakin appointed a second Victorian.[5] In 1912, after the death of Justice O'Connor, three more took their place on the Bench appointed by the Fisher Labor Government. Drawn from Victoria, New South Wales and Queensland, there again was no South Australian. South Australia's influence on the Court's decisions and the shape of the Constitution relied on intervention as a litigant (usually unsuccessfully).

Intercolonial trade and financial arrangements

Although the abolition of tariffs and duties between the states had considerable revenue implications, these had been replaced by an obligation on the Commonwealth to guarantee a share of such revenues. A limitation clause meant that the requirement could be cancelled after ten years, and this occurred despite the complaints of the states. As the Commonwealth reserved more revenue for its own purposes, Commonwealth financial dominance was increasing but this was not yet fully apparent. The ability to raise loan funds under the aegis of the Commonwealth was of benefit in the London market, and South Australia had taken full advantage of this.

Overall the ability to trade freely and export without penalty within Australia served South Australia well. For agricultural products, while the state lost its tobacco industry, it had success with wine. The ability to continue to protect this industry against pests such as phylloxera and fruit fly remained despite the broad wording of the free trade power. The state's nascent manufacturing industry had done better than other states', particularly supplying the needs of gold miners in Western Australia, and Federation consolidated the ability to operate in such markets.

Immigration control and the development of the Northern Territory

South Australia, like Queensland, had long been faced with a dilemma on the issue of northern development and productivity. Since 1863 it had responsibility for the Territory and many great schemes and development possibilities had been conceived. Much had been spent, but the great mineral Eldorado, the booming tropical produce, the grazing industry, and transport through and beyond the centre to the north had all come to nothing.[6] The greatest achievement had been the successful completion of the Overland Telegraph Line, not to be undervalued, as it made South Australia the communications hub of the continent. It was an extraordinary enterprise, but the spin-offs in regional northern development did not follow.

The prevailing view was that 'white man' could not work productively in the tropics. Only by importing 'native' labour could development take place – the South Sea Islanders (Kanakas) in the Queensland sugar industry, the Chinese and southern Indians (Tamils) in Darwin, and the Japanese in the Broome pearl industry were all examples. The recruitment of

Indian labour to Fiji (a fellow member in the 1880s of the Federal Council of Australasia) was another example.

The problem was that the south was resolutely opposed to the entry, or even presence, of 'coloured' workers in their colonial economies. From the time of the gold rush in Victoria the Chinese, in particular, were seen as a cheap alternative to dignified labour and good working conditions, undercutting wages and conditions for all. There was a strong racist streak in this thinking, but not all of it was prejudice; radical and conservative joined in fearing that the labour market would be swamped and the security of the colonies compromised by the rising power of the East, particularly Japan. Imperial policy, faced with issues in India, South Africa and the Pacific, was at odds with the Australian position. Britain formed an alliance with Japan and would not allow discrimination against its citizens in the Empire. This made the colonies more strident and assertive. In 1888 a major conference on the issue, precipitated by the Playford and Kingston Government, attempted to reach a common agreement on what was later called the White Australia Policy. Federation offered the best way to enforce a policy binding on the whole continent that could prevent expedient deviations in the interest of northern development. It is no surprise that the Immigration Restriction Act of 1901 was one of the first measures passed by the new federal parliament.

South Australia felt that the Territory would always be a burden on the State Treasury. A national government could address the defence needs of the north, was the only level of government capable of backing and financing a northern railway, and could take responsibility for its Indigenous population. The majority in South Australia wanted to get rid of the Territory, and so it is not surprising that as soon as Tom

Price and the Labor-Liberal coalition took office it was made a priority. The process took time, one of the issues being how much compensation the Commonwealth should pay to South Australia for its fruitless expenditure on the Territory in attempts to administer and develop it over nearly fifty years. Another was how to embed the promise to build a north-south railway link in the transfer agreement. Eventually agreement was reached. The six million pounds that South Australia received in compensation, although reckoned at less than half what had been spent, was nevertheless a significant contribution to the Treasury. The undertaking to build the railway was incorporated – although, fatally, without a time commitment for commencement or completion. Transfer took place in 1911, and although there were some who regretted the cession, for most this was seen as a major gain from Federation.

Transport hub

The vision of South Australia at the head of a great network of railways spanning the continent, supplemented by a permanently navigable Murray River system terminating in South Australia, was strongly alive in the first years of Federation. In the case of Western Australia, a reluctant participant in the Commonwealth, the east-west railway was seen as non-negotiable, although it took a decade to start the real work. Meanwhile, despite South Australian expenditure on its side of the border to extend the existing line north, there was still no progress on the north-south link when war was declared.

South Australia had always seen the River Murray as one of its great potential economic generators. Its value as a means of transport was enhanced by the irrigation settlements pioneered in the 1880s. When the Chaffey brothers were experiencing problems with Victoria in developing Mildura in 1885, the Downer Government had seized the initiative, inviting them to undertake what became the Renmark project in South Australia. Since then successive South Australian Governments had put a lot of energy and resources into irrigation projects, including the partly failed experiment of the Village Settlements during the 1890s economic depression.

The schemes of settlement and production in all the riparian states should have enhanced plans for the river as a great inland highway for goods and passengers, but Victoria and New South Wales built railways from the coast to carry the trade and by-pass the river. This made sense as the uncertain seasonal flow of the river made transport unreliable. In 1902 the Murray actually ceased to flow for only the second time since South Australia's European settlement. How to deal with the river was one of the biggest issues of dispute at the Constitutional Convention. South Australia, the end user, wanted the Commonwealth to have the ultimate say, but was defeated by New South Wales and Victoria, which claimed 'riparian rights'. The best that could be done was the insertion of a reference to the right of 'reasonable use of the waters', moved by Downer – the effect of which is still to be properly tested in the High Court.

Following the failure to resolve the issue at the Convention, South Australia had no choice but to try to get the other states involved in agreements (this had been going on since the Intercolonial Conference of 1863) and if possible for the Commonwealth, with its financial resources, to also come to the party. Despite the long history of failure to agree on works that would provide storage for the maintenance of river flow in bad seasons and locks to guarantee that much of it was navigable, breakthroughs had occurred by the eve of war. In 1913 an

Interstate Conference of Engineers came up with proposals for locks and weirs to do the job. The Commonwealth agreed to be a partner, taking national responsibility and promising to financially contribute to the works. The agreement had still not been concluded at the outbreak of war but the urgency of action was underlined by the 1914 drought, which again saw the river cease to flow. South Australian could feel confident that something would definitely go ahead, as indeed it did from 1915.

New federal powers

New powers acquired by the federal government included what is now known as social security, but was then thought of as old age pensions or 'national insurance', and conciliation and arbitration of industrial disputes.

The pensions power was proposed by South Australia's James Howe against strong opposition, but he was finally successful in the last session of the Federal Convention in Melbourne in 1898. The mobility of the Australian population was one of the strongest arguments he used to make it a federal responsibility.[7] South Australia had not introduced a pension, unlike some other states, pending the Commonwealth exercising its power in this area. It was vindicated when the universal system was introduced by the Deakin Government and means-tested age pensions were paid from 1909, with disability pensions the following year.

The other major innovation, this time the brainchild of Kingston, was the granting of the power of the Commonwealth to settle industrial disputes of an interstate character. The resulting conciliation and arbitration system, established in its original form in 1904, was unique to Australia and proved robust and flexible over most of the twentieth century. By the eve of war most trade unions and employers' organisations were using the system. The landmark minimum wage ruling of Justice Higgins in 1907 was seen not just as an industrial provision, but as a major social reform.

Charles Cameron Kingston in 1890.
[SLSA B 1848]

In summary, the South Australian delegates could be well satisfied with their work and influence on the shape of the Constitution. Its implementation in the years up to the First World War could be seen as vindicating this. The overall balance sheet of Federation could be seen as working well for South Australia and its objectives on the eve of war. It was only after the conflict that its many inadequacies were perceived.

The political situation: federal and state

War was declared in Europe on 4 August 1914, at a time when Australia had a caretaker government. A double dissolution of the federal parliament took place on 30 July 1914 and election day was set for 5 September. It was seen as one of the most important federal elections until then, as the deadlock-breaking measure was being used for the first time. The campaign took place during the first month of the war. The election resulted in a clear victory for the Labor Party led by Andrew Fisher, returning after a term from 1910 to 1913. Fisher was sworn in as prime minister on 17 September 1914.

The early years of Federation had been a time of political instability, with the so-called 'three elevens' (the Free Traders, the Protectionists and the Labor Party) battling for federal supremacy. With the 'Fusion' of the first two in 1909 to form the Liberal Party, two-party contests became the norm.

The situation had been more complex at the state level. The 'minimalist' model of Federation was still seen to be embodied in the Constitution, and the reality of increasing Commonwealth prominence was only slowly becoming apparent. A number of leading South Australian politicians had left South Australia for the federal scene, and a number of those remaining in state politics initially had federal aspirations. Of the seven South Australian members of the House of Representatives elected in 1901, six were sitting state members of parliament, including three former premiers. Four of them had been Convention delegates. They had been a formidable presence in all parties or factions in the House of Assembly. The Senate similarly became the destination for talent and experience from South Australia. Five of the six initial South Australian members were from the colonial parliament. Three had been federal delegates, and two were also former premiers. With the exception of Downer and Solomon, both of whom returned to state politics after 1903, the South Australians went on to have distinguished and influential federal careers, although never attaining the office of prime minister. But a lot of talent had left the local political scene.

It is also worth noting that eight sitting members of state parliament stood unsuccessfully for federal parliament, continuing as local members after 1901. Most surprising was the candidature of one of the chief anti-federalists, the leader of the Labor Party, Tom Price, who had been so prominent in his opposition to Federation and the Constitution Bill. His biographer says that he was motivated by the need to get as many 'straight Labor into the national arena as possible'.[8] Four Labor men were chosen by party plebiscite to stand, two, including Price, for the Representatives, and two for the Senate. Price was unsuccessful. His failure to enter federal parliament was to prove very significant for the course of politics in South Australia between Federation and Price's untimely death in 1909.

Whatever was hoped about the continuing significance and role of the state in the Commonwealth, it was clear where the aspirations of the political leaders lay. A new generation of local state leaders was needed among all parties and factions in what were very difficult economic transitional times, but the pool of experience had been greatly reduced.

One way of dealing with the exodus of talent was to acknowledge the fact that Federation would make the task of government smaller at state level, and consequently the Assembly and Council numbers were reduced, as was the ministry. A major re-drawing of electoral boundaries was needed for the Assembly, as numbers shrank from 54 to 42, while the Council was reduced from 24 to 20. The traditional six ministers were replaced by four. Otherwise it was business as usual in the parliament, where the biggest issue remained the deadlock between the House of Assembly and the Legislative Council over the Council's limited property franchise. The unbending Council was not affected by the new status of the colony nor the changes in its numbers.

Most Free Traders and Protectionists grouped under the broader umbrella of the conservative Australian Defence League (ADL) while others were still of liberal or independent persuasion. The country members were also divided in their affiliations. The United Labor Party had experienced some division but basically was intact, if small in numbers. With the departure of the federal members, a new ministry was formed in May 1901, headed by John Jenkins, a long-term member of the Kingston and Holder Cabinets. Two other former Kingston ministers, one of whom had been a Convention delegate, provided continuity, but the ministry had a more conservative cast.

The first post-Federation election was held for the reduced House of Assembly in May 1902.[9] Jenkins and his supporters secured 20 seats and retained government with the tacit support of the Labor Party's five members. Labor did badly in the reduced House, losing half its numbers, while the ADL bloc increased its representation with 17 seats, becoming the official opposition. It is interesting to note that forty of the members of the previous House were elected, while only 13 failed. Hardly any new blood had been introduced into the new state legislature. Jenkins and Butler provided continuity in the ministry until 1905, while seven others came and went. During the term the ministry became more conservative and ready to deal with the ADL, alienating Labor and some of its more progressive supporters. In 1905 Jenkins appointed himself to the position of agent-general in London. Richard Butler formed an even more conservative ministry that, after an election in May 1905, was defeated in the House after five months of office.

Discussion had taken place on the formation of a coalition between Labor's Tom Price and the progressive Liberals led by Archibald Peake. Peake was confident that his group would hold more seats than Labor, and it was agreed that this would determine who was premier. Meanwhile the conservatives had split between the ADL and a new country party, the Farmers and Producers Political Union (FPPU). The 1905 result was a Labor triumph, increasing its numbers to 15, which, with Peake's seven, gave the coalition a majority. Price claimed his right to the premiership, the second Labor man in any Australian state (or colony) to hold the office.[10] Alarm from many sections of the press and public about a socialist holding the office was quickly allayed. The ministry was divided between the two partners, with Price and Kirkpatrick from Labor, and Peake – as Treasurer – and Laurence O'Loughlin (a veteran of Kingston's ministry) from the Liberals. Price and Kirkpatrick were given leave by Labor not to attend caucus meetings, to demonstrate that they would not be subject to direction from the party, and were excused from the pledge. At the end of 1908 the Cabinet was increased to six but the balance maintained. This coalition survived unchallenged, increasing its majority in the election of November 1906, caused by deadlock with the Council, until Tom Price's death at the end of May 1909.

Two more elections were held before 1914. Reflecting the 'Fusion' between Free Traders and Protectionists at the federal level in the face of the rising power of Labor, Peake dissolved the coalition after Price's death and became leader of a united conservative party called the Liberal Union. The election of April

1910 was the first two-party contest, setting the pattern for the ensuing years. After winning easily in 1910 under John Verran, Labor continued to face a hostile Legislative Council in which it was hopelessly outnumbered due to the restricted franchise. The Council felt confident enough to cause a constitutional crisis by threatening to block supply, and insisting on unacceptable amendments to the Budget in February 1912. It was able to force Labor to the polls that same year. There were over 20 per cent more voters on the roll for this election but the results of 1910 were reversed. Although Peake held a comfortable majority by 1914, Labor was on track to defeat him in the elections the following year.

In summary, with the transition from colony to state the powers and activities of the ministry and the state legislature had diminished. This was not necessarily evident to the practitioners, despite their scramble for federal office. The stable two-party system, with the two sides alternating as economic and political circumstances dictated, seemed to be well-established in South Australia by 1914, and the electorate, despite the campaigns of the conservative press, no longer held fears of the 'socialist' Labor Party in government.

Economic conditions

Federation certainly did not bring immediate prosperity to South Australia, nor to the rest of the country.[11] The great Federation Drought that peaked in 1902 was devastating in its impact on rural production. The worst rainfall in South Australia since 1891 was matched, as stated previously, by the Murray ceasing to flow for only the second time since European settlement. Recovery took four years. Very good rains in 1906, 1908, 1909 (the highest recorded) and 1910 got the state back on its feet. After those first few years, South Australia, and the new nation, enjoyed a surge of prosperity which continued almost until the eve of war. Population grew solidly, a factor not just of the birthrate (which increased considerably) but also the flow of immigrants from interstate and overseas.

A good indicator of economic health and prosperity was the net migration number, which became positive, boosted by the re-introduction of government-assisted immigration in several states. This positive change and the accompanying economic growth made South Australia more comfortable with Federation and seemed to confirm its overall benefit. What was also significant was the expansion of Adelaide and its industries and employment opportunities over this period. The census of 1901 saw rural areas and regional towns with a total population not much less than the capital. By 1911 most of the increase in population had been absorbed by a burgeoning Adelaide.

South Australia entered 1914 in very good shape. But by the end of the year it was having to put men and resources into the war effort, while experiencing a massive drought, with the lowest rainfall ever recorded and the Murray again drying up.

Experience of war

The citizens of South Australia were told by caretaker Prime Minister Cook, with the unequivocal endorsement of his pending successor Andrew Fisher, that they would be joining Britain in the war against Germany and her allies in August 1914. They would not have been surprised, not only because of the imperial connection and the consequent assumption that the thirteen-year-old Commonwealth would be at Britain's side, but also because of two comparatively recent precedents. On the eve of Federation, while South Australia was still a self-governing colony, it and the other Australian colonies had volunteered locally raised contingents to fight in the South African War or Boer War (1899–1902). When the Commonwealth was established on 1 January 1901 the Boer War was still in progress, and it soon took over defence matters from the states, resulting in the forces becoming an Australian rather than a colonial responsibility. And in 1900 South Australia's single naval vessel, HMCS *Protector*, was sent to join the expedition in China to help suppress the Boxer Rebellion and defend imperial interests there.

The Boer War has been largely forgotten because the scale of the First World War overwhelmed it in popular memory. But on the eve of war in 1914, memories of the Boer War were sharper, and it was the only conflict to provide a precedent as to how events might unfold in Europe and throughout the Empire. Unlike the situation in 1914, there had been the prospect of war in South Africa over some years, beginning in 1895 with the notorious 'Jameson Raid'. Many Australians were working in the mines in the Transvaal and joining in demonstrations of grievance against Paul Kruger's government. The Australian colonies were preoccupied with Federation and internal matters and not inclined to involve themselves in the issue, despite petitions to do so.

By 1899, as war in South Africa became more certain, the attitude of the colonial governments remained equivocal. The British Government was very confident that any war would be short and sharp and that less well-trained colonial volunteers from the colonies would possibly get in the way of the regular troops from the United Kingdom, but they wanted the Empire to demonstrate support, and the Colonial Secretary, Joseph Chamberlain, sought a 'spontaneous' offer of troops, for symbolic as much as military reasons.[12]

Chamberlain used one of his confidants in Australia, the newly appointed Governor of South Australia, Lord Tennyson, to sound out his colleagues and help to induce the 'spontaneous' offer of support. Premier Kingston canvassed the South Australian Cabinet and the initial response was negative. A further approach resulted in the more positive response that Cabinet might support a volunteer force. Chamberlain enthusiastically welcomed this and other supporting declarations from the colonies, although they fell well short of being offers, and when war was declared in October all the colonies received a telegram advising of 'acceptance' of their offers, detailing numbers and manner of raising separate colonial units. The troops were dispersed among the British Army in South Africa, and Australia contributed mounted riflemen or light horse, which proved to be of considerable military value over the course of the war. Parliamentary approval was necessary in all the colonies and was secured with few dissenters or sceptics, most members succumbing to a wave of imperial patriotism that came after the declaration. Only in South Australia were real difficulties experienced, principally in the Legislative Council, where the President's casting vote was needed to pass the motion. It was felt 'German' sympathies for Kruger's republic may have been an influence in South Australian attitudes.

The war began very badly for the British, with some spectacular defeats, which transferred public attitudes from apathy, or, in some quarters, sympathy for the farmers' cause, to one of patriotic support of an Empire under unexpected threat. Public enthusiasm in South Australia resulted in huge crowds gathering for the send-off of the first contingent on 2 November 1899. An offer of further troops was made while the first contingents were still at sea, which was accepted and encouraged from London. The war now dominated the news and the Siege of Mafeking was seen as a make-or-break moment. Mafeking was relieved on 17 May 1900 and was celebrated in the streets of Adelaide with demonstrations, fireworks, parties and eventually public drunkenness and riots. This was probably the zenith of support for the Boer War.

Crowds line King William Street, Adelaide, in 1902 to watch a parade of returned soldiers from the Boer War.
[SLSA B 61260]

After the Boer War ended in 1902 there was no commemoration day proclaimed either by state or Commonwealth governments, although memorials were erected in some towns and cities, including a striking statue of a horseman in front of Government House in Adelaide. The returned men, after initial big receptions, spent the next decade arguing about pay entitlements, pensions and rehabilitation services. Some of these claims had not been settled by the outbreak of the First World War.

On a population basis South Australia had made a significant contribution the Boer War. The first South Australian contingent, comprising 127 infantry and mounted rifles, left on 2 November 1899 and returned after twelve months in action that saw five deaths, two in action and three from disease. This was the first of six contingents of troops totalling over 1000 men, of whom 46 did not return, an equal number due to death from action as to disease. A group of nine nurses led by Sister Bidmead left in mid-February 1900 and served for two years, returning within three months of the end of the war without casualties. South Australians were also part of four of the Commonwealth contingents, three of them Commonwealth Horse and one a medical team.

In August 1914 South Australians still expected to fight beside Britain, under their own commanders and units, and as volunteers not conscripts. They may have assumed the war would be over sooner than that of South Africa, and that it would be a war of cavalry movement and field guns. The massive catastrophe of 1914–1918 dwarfed and extinguished memories and even awareness of the impact of the earlier conflict for succeeding generations, kept alive only through the controversy surrounding Breaker Morant.

In summary, despite the drought and the war, 1914 was still

a time of optimism, based on the years of prosperity that had preceded it, the tangible overall benefits of Federation, and the belief that the war would be over quickly and victoriously, leaving South Australia relatively untouched. The reality of the following years would be shocking and vastly different.

3

New women and the modern family *Continuity and change in pre-war domestic life*

MARGARET ANDERSON AND ALISON MACKINNON

Just before Christmas in 1909 Gertrude Lewis finally married her fiancé of three and a half years, James Anderson. They went off on honeymoon to Point Sturt on Lake Alexandrina, before returning to the city in the New Year to set up house together.[1] Apart from their rather extended engagement, there was nothing particularly unusual about this start to married life. But in fact their marriage was to be anything but conventional. For Lavinia Gertrude Lewis (always known as Gertrude, or Gertie) was one of South Australia's 'new women'. When she married in 1909 she already had an established career – a career she maintained throughout her marriage and subsequent maternity.

Gertie was born in 1884 in the comfortable middle-class suburb of Goodwood Park and had a fairly privileged upbringing. Her father was an Unley town councillor and, along with her two younger sisters, Gertie was sent to the Unley Park School, run by the Misses Thornber. There, in 1900 and 1901, she won the first of many prizes, an 'essay prize' and, in a pointer to her later career, prizes for 'elocution'.[2] They were substantial prizes – complete leather-bound sets of Shakespeare and the works of Alfred, Lord Tennyson. The family still has some of them. From there Gertie and her younger sister Irene went to the University

Lavinia Gertrude Lewis, always known as Gertrude or Gertie, in 1907, aged 22. Gertie had a tinted version made into a brooch. [*Observer*, 2 February 1907]

of Adelaide, where Gertie graduated with a Bachelor of Arts, while her sister read science. Gertie continued to compete in elocution competitions with considerable success. In 1905 she took out the main prize at the prestigious Ballarat Eisteddfod, and it was there that she probably met her future husband – by then a prize-winning elocutionist in his own right and a notable competition judge, living in Ballarat. They became engaged in June 1906 – the beginning of a long personal, professional and creative partnership that continued until his death in 1945.[3] The family story has it that Gertie insisted James move to Adelaide from Ballarat, and certainly by mid-1908 they were performing together on a regular basis, both in Adelaide and in various regional centres.[4] Both continued to compete and adjudicate in Ballarat and Melbourne annually but their income came from teaching elocution, and later from their practice in the new discipline of speech therapy.[5] It was lucrative enough to enable them to build a substantial house in the Adelaide foothills during the 1930s.

Two children only were born to the marriage, some eleven years apart, in 1910 and 1921, although there were stories of miscarriages in between. Gertie maintained her practice throughout this period, employing a housekeeper cum nanny to care for the children. She continued to teach speech and drama and to practise as a speech therapist right up until her death in the late 1950s. On the eve of war we find Gertie and James living with their small son, Val, in the comfortable suburb of Unley, making regular appearances in local theatres and in regional towns.[6] They led busy, and by all accounts satisfying, and creative lives.

The modern family

It might be said that Mr and Mrs James Anderson epitomised the 'modern' family of the twentieth century. Certainly they led very different lives from those of their parents. In the previous 30 years the nature of family life had changed extensively, both in South Australia and in most of the western world. The most profound change was in the overall size of the family. From about the 1870s in South Australia marital fertility fell precipitously and continued to fall into the early decades of the new century. Previous studies by both Mackinnon and Anderson have shown that completed marital fertility fell from an average of eight births in the mid-nineteenth century, to an average of four by 1900, with the decline continuing into the 1920s.[7] Educated women like Gertie had consistently lower fertility than others, a trend that caused considerable concern among the new ranks of eugenicists and social statisticians, who accused such women of selfishly contributing to 'race suicide'.[8] Of course the decline in family size was not universal. It is in the nature of statistical averages to gloss over the variations in experience that characterise human populations. But the trend was widely dispersed. Anderson has argued elsewhere that the trend towards smaller families in South Australia was evident across all the traditional divides of class, region and religious affiliation, whatever variations there might have been within each group.[9] It was this new, much smaller family that saw its sons off to war in 1914 and that bore the brunt of the terrible losses that followed.

The period of 1880 to 1921 was a critical one in changing both the material circumstances of women's lives and accepted notions of femininity. For middle-class women the decline in infant mortality, improvements in sanitation and the provision of gas, electricity and household appliances introduced the possibility of looking for an occupation outside of the household and organising domestic staff. This, and the shorter span of child rearing, presented a very different pattern to everyday life, to married life – and to women's lives within marriage. For a small bunch of highly educated women, the tiny band who had graduated from the University of Adelaide by 1914 (or those who had studied a few subjects), the possibilities of work and profession meant that far fewer married. Indeed of all women who had graduated from the University of Adelaide by 1922 (200), almost 50 per cent did not marry. This high rate of spinsterhood was not war-related. Rather these were 'new women' who entered professions, taught in girls' schools and urged young women to expand their horizons. Those who married did so at a later stage than the norm and produced, on average, fewer children. Their marital lives were clearly precursors of what was to come.[10]

Just how this reduction in family size was effected is still a matter for debate among historians and historical demographers, since there was no significant advance in the technology of birth control that might explain it at this time. There were various mechanical means of contraception, including condoms,pessaries – both purchased and home-made – sponges, which could be soaked in solutions reputed to have a spermicidal effect (lemon juice was one), and, from about the 1890s, the rubber diaphragm or Dutch cap.[11] These all acted as physical barriers and were more or less effective, depending on how they were fitted and used. They could be purchased in Adelaide from chemists, or by mail order, and were advertised more or less openly in the daily press – albeit with the heavy use of euphemism.[12] Many households in Australia were also said to possess a Higginson's syringe, which could be used to douche after intercourse, but it is fair to say that none of these methods was consistently reliable and all, except the diaphragm, had been in existence for generations, without noticeable effect.

We have concluded that the most likely underlying explanation for what demographers have called the 'quiet revolution' was cultural. Increasingly, ordinary people came to believe that the large, unregulated families of the past were passé, inconsistent with a modern, civilized society – even, increasingly, a source of embarrassment – and they modified their sexual behaviour accordingly.[13] In the self-consciously modern nation of Australia in the 1900s, unregulated fertility was no longer seen as desirable. One article published in the

Mail in March 1913 quoted the eminent British doctor Ramsay-Smith: 'the trend of civilisation must always be in the direction of smaller families ... a state whose population continues to increase in obedience to unchecked instinct can progress only from bad to worse'.[14] But as is often the case, there was a wide spectrum of views on the subject. Debate continued about the degree of restraint deemed acceptable, and on the dangers of declining fertility in a young nation like Australia, with its wide-open spaces and small population. When the extent of fertility decline was first publicized in the late 1890s and early 1900s there was a good deal of moral panic about potential 'race suicide' and the 'selfishness' of married women, who were accused of shirking their maternal duty to the nation. However, even at the height of concern in the early 1900s, there was an underlying note of resignation in the commentary. In 1903 the South Australian Registrar of Births, Deaths and Marriages, a careful statistician, presented this somewhat awkward summary of the situation as he saw it. It was a delicate subject and he was clearly at pains to avoid giving offence.

> It is believed, though this department can offer no undoubted proof ... that in recent years some – perhaps a good many – of the married people of the state have preferred to have small or, at any rate, not large families, and have in consequence had recourse to various means to restrict the number of their offspring.[15]

As for ordinary South Australians, they went right on doing, quietly, what they had been doing for a generation by then, and ignored the statisticians and moral commentators. As is often the case, the cartoonists may have captured the mood of the people more accurately than the pompous social commentators.

One fairly typical small cartoon published in the *Critic*, an illustrated Adelaide weekly, in September 1899 shows a horrified father confronting huge triplets. Captioned cheekily 'Keeping His End Up', the cartoonist has his 'Startled Father' exclaim: 'Great Snakes – Triplets. And those blanky idiots at the census office complain about decrease of the birth rate'.[16]

But based on the current state of contraceptive development, achieving smaller families was not without its problems.

A humorous take on contemporary concerns at the fall of the birth rate, with, for the time, a slightly risqué by-line.
[*Critic*, 16 September 1899]

Demographers have concluded that the most common form of contraception in use within marriage was probably withdrawal, which had the great advantage of being cheap, but which also relied absolutely on the cooperation of the male partner and on considerable self-control at the appropriate moment.[17] It might have been combined with more or less extended periods of abstinence, but abstinence has never been a very popular form of birth control. Both methods had the potential to increase the level of tension in a marriage, especially if the husband was a reluctant participant. This was a period of considerable reticence in sexual matters, but we can see occasional hints of the pressures involved in these intimate negotiations, sometimes in unlikely sources.[18]

Sadly the desire to have fewer children had a dark side for women as well. It is very difficult to assess the extent to which married women resorted to the abortionist to free themselves of ‘unwanted obstructions’ and ‘restore regularity’, as the careful advertisements often put it. Janet McCalman has argued that the Royal Women’s Hospital in Melbourne saw a marked increase in admissions for septic abortions in these decades.[19] The implication of her study is that class was the chief factor in play here and that wealthy women found it easier to find a sympathetic doctor who would perform a discreet (and safe) curette in a private hospital. But less privileged women could not afford the fees of such expensive treatment. In desperation at repeated pregnancies some sought the services of one or other of the abortionists known to have operated in Adelaide at this time. One notorious abortionist, Madam Harper (or Harpur), was active in the city through the decades of the 1890s and 1900s. She was tried for murder twice but only convicted (of the lesser charge of manslaughter) once.[20]

Madam Harper was not the only abortionist working in Adelaide, but typically their activities only came to light when their hapless patients died. From the accounts of these cases published in the press it is clear that most of the women who sought the clandestine services of what we now call 'backyard abortionists' were single women, desperate on finding themselves pregnant outside marriage. It may be too that these terminations were late-term abortions and hence doubly risky. Typically the young women who found themselves 'in the family way', or in what the press usually described as 'in a certain condition', tried first to persuade their young men to marry them. Sometimes it is clear from their dying accounts that the men in question had held out the prospect of marriage, only to renege once its likelihood became a reality. The young women then resorted to the range of popular remedies for unwanted pregnancies – hot baths, various pills and potions (most of which were purges of greater or lesser ferocity), douches and even self-administered syringes or other instruments. It was only when these failed that they sought out the abortionist. Abortions were not cheap for working girls. Mrs Clara Laker, who was tried for the willful murder of Alma Kure in April 1913, charged two guineas for the procedure that was performed at her home in Goodwood.[21] Madam Harper charged a similar fee. Typically the operation involved inserting an instrument into the uterus and leaving it in place until a miscarriage began. The young woman was almost always sent away at this point, with no further supervision. Alma Kure took a married friend with her to see Mrs Laker: others went alone, sometimes travelling from regional South Australia into Adelaide where the city offered anonymity.

Why did these young women take such dreadful risks? There were alternatives – a supervised delivery in the lying-in hospital of the Destitute Asylum in Kintore Avenue was one. But it is clear from the many accounts in the newspapers that the common reason was the social disgrace that inevitably followed an unwed pregnancy.[22] Social attitudes to women were changing in South Australia at this time, but the double standard of sexual morality was to linger for many decades yet. When the much-heralded Queen Victoria Maternity Home opened with great fanfare in 1902, it reserved its pristine modern facilities for respectably married women.[23] A 'ladies' committee' interviewed all applicants for admission, just to make sure.[24]

Other desperate young women managed to conceal their pregnancies and give birth alone, disposing of their infants afterwards. Generally these babies were born alive but were either smothered, or in one case strangled, immediately afterwards and then buried. All of the cases reported came to light because neighbours or other household members became suspicious and called the police. These women might have been charged with murder, like the abortionists, but almost always they faced the lesser charge of 'concealment of birth', even where the medical evidence clearly indicated that the child had been born alive. There was obviously a good deal of sympathy for these women, alongside the evident disapproval. The same sympathy may have extended in some way to the abortionists, none of whom was convicted of murder. Juries were notoriously reluctant to convict in these cases, partly, no doubt, because murder at this time was a capital offence.

Often the young men involved in these affairs were unknown, or at least unnamed, but occasionally they were called to give evidence, and in one instance at least the jury at a coroner's inquest made a point of registering their disgust at the man's callous abandonment of his partner. Lucy Knaggs of Norwood was charged with concealment of birth after the body of her infant was found buried in a garden in Kensington in April 1900. She described the birth of the baby as a 'miscarriage' and insisted that it was born dead. Lucy told the police that she had been 'keeping company' with Alfred Waples for some 18 months and that he had promised to marry her. In dismissing the case, the jury said that 'there was nothing to show the cause of death and added a rider desiring that the coroner should severely censure the witness Waples for his heartless conduct, and for the reluctant manner in which he gave his evidence'.[25] This may have given Lucy and her family some sense of justice, although it was small recompense for the trauma and social disgrace.

These are just a few of the many similar cases reported in the press in the years before the First World War. Such trials were notable public spectacles. Courts were invariably crowded and the newspapers reported each case in great detail, summarising each piece of evidence and identifying and describing each witness. Similar cases from outside the state were also reported, creating a repetitive narrative theme of betrayal, desperation and disgrace. This may have served as a warning to some women to guard their chastity at all costs: equally it may have alerted others to the possibility of escaping a desperate predicament. Either way, it is obvious from many of the cases heard in these years that there was a well-established network of knowledge existing below the surface of 'respectable' Adelaide.

Continuity and change

These cases, and others like them, hint at the many continuities of experience for women in South Australia in these decades, in stark contrast to the lives of middle-class women like Gertie. It is true that much had changed for women, both inside and outside marriage. In 1895 women were at last full citizens, able to vote on equal terms with men and to stand for election, although this last provision was initially contested when Catherine Helen Spence stood for election to the Federal Convention in 1897.[26] Significant amendments to the Married Women's Property Acts in the 1880s also improved the capacity of married women to control and manage their own property, but in other respects South Australia lagged behind the other states. The double sexual standard continued to hamper attempts to equalise divorce laws for women, despite the efforts of groups like the Women's Non-Party Political Association, formed in 1909, with Catherine Helen Spence as its first president. In her foundation address, Spence outlined the Association's commitment to 'equal Federal marriage and divorce laws', a cause she had championed personally for 30 years, but there was no appetite for reform in the state parliament. Helen Jones speculated in 1986 that South Australia's family-based founding ethos might help to explain this particular reluctance to liberalise divorce for women.[27] Similarly, women continued to suffer many other legal inequalities within marriage. They had no automatic right to any property of the marriage and attempts to equalise inheritance laws failed in the parliament in 1908.[28] Fathers retained most of their custodial rights over any children of the marriage in other than 'exceptional circumstances', giving them absolute authority to determine religion, schooling, work and punishment, or to grant, or withhold, permission to marry, if they chose to exercise it. By 1914, however, a widow did at least become guardian of her children automatically on her husband's death.[29] Meanwhile a husband could, and sometimes did, will all of 'his' property away from his wife, even in apparently blameless circumstances.

When the noted philanthropist Dr William Wyatt died in Adelaide in 1886, he left all of his substantial fortune to a trust, leaving his wife of 50 years dependent on its trustees' benevolence.

Inside the home there was a similar story of some advances, but much continuity. The advent of the gas stove was probably the single most liberating appliance for the housewife at this time. But it is difficult to know how many households had gas stoves installed and certainly many still cooked on the labour-intensive, hot, wood-fuelled variety, especially outside the city. An article in the *Advertiser* in February 1912 implied that 'many households' in the city were waiting for the new stoves, which, according to the Secretary of the South Australian Gas Company, were 'becoming increasingly popular. Housewives who have difficulty in securing domestic help', he said, 'find them very convenient'.[30] There was also a kerosene-fuelled stove that was marketed to country areas, but it was a bit inclined to explode.[31] In fact, wood stoves continued to dominate the advertisements of the period, and local companies like Simpsons did not even begin to manufacture gas stoves until the 1920s.[32] Other aspects of housework remained much as they had been in the previous century – labour-intensive, heavy and hot work. The family wash was still an all-day affair, involving boiling coppers, heavy lifting through hand-turned wringers, and much starching and bluing. The technology of irons, similarly, had changed little. Most still heated on stove tops and were of heavy, cast iron construction. New women, like Gertie, had little choice but to employ domestic help if they wanted the 'freedom' to work outside the home, but finding suitable domestics was increasingly difficult. Not surprisingly, many women preferred alternative occupations, in manufacturing, in retail and in the newer occupations of typewriting and telephony. The 46 per cent of women who listed their occupations as domestic servants in 1901 had declined to 36 per cent by 1911.[33] The writing was on the wall.

Changing fashions

One more intimate aspect of women's lives that did improve in these years was their dress. In the late nineteenth century, as women advanced slowly and painfully towards emancipation, the prevailing fashions had become, if anything, more restrictive. The huge crinoline skirts of mid-century gave way in the 1870s and 1880s to increasingly fitted skirts, drawn tightly over waist and hips, draped at the back over bustles of horsehair or steel, and held in place by intricate arrangements of tapes and fastenings. Close-fitting bodices encased the body, and collars grew higher and more rigid, encircling the neck. Both bodices and collars were shaped by insertions of whalebone or steel. Under the bodice was yet more whalebone, in corsets that confined the body from bust to hip. The frills and apparent looseness of women's blouses and bodices in the early 1900s were illusions, consisting of frilled and gathered outer layers, stitched to boned, close-fitting underbodices.

Detailed fashion notes appeared regularly in Adelaide's newspapers, often accompanied by careful line drawings. [*Daily Herald*, 25 November 1911]

From about 1910 women's dress became more relaxed in style. The tight waists and high collars disappeared, replaced by more loosely fitted, long tunics worn over narrow under-skirts, which rose to ankle-length. A short-lived and rather silly fashion for very narrow skirts, known as hobble skirts, entertained cartoonists briefly in the years between about 1910 and 1913, but was soon abandoned.[34] Hobble skirts impeded even normal walking and made stepping up into tramcars and carriages all but impossible. There were calls, probably tongue-in-cheek, for Adelaide's tramcars to be modified to accommodate this fashion trend but, no doubt to the relief of the Tramways Trust, fashion moved on, and women could walk, once again, without hobbling.[35] In the years before the war women's undergarments also relaxed somewhat, although the many layers persisted. A typical set of underclothing included a sleeveless chemise, wide-legged drawers, a corset, corset cover (or camisole) and one or two long, frilled petticoats, tied or buttoned at the waist. But the corsets were no longer laced quite so tightly, allowing more freedom of movement than before.

South Australian women were kept up to date by a steady stream of fashion articles in the local newspapers. By the early 1900s these articles were illustrated with carefully detailed line drawings, although photographs of real women were less common. There were exceptions, of course. A photograph of 'Mrs. (Dr.) Booth' of Broken Hill was published by the *Mail* on Saturday 26 July 1913, adjacent to a lengthy article by 'Irene' on 'Fresh Designs in Blouses'. Mrs Booth was described as 'well known in social life at Broken Hill. A great advocate for children's playing spaces' – a hint, perhaps, that the newspapers were beginning to provide more than endless fashion notes for their female readers. But the fashion notes remained predominant. 'Irene', who wrote for the Adelaide *Mail*, gave detailed descriptions of style, individual garments, materials and all manner of trimmings for her readers, accompanied by advice about the trends she predicted most likely to prevail.[36] There were descriptions of the toilettes of real women too, observed at society weddings and civic receptions.[37] From these accounts we can conclude that South Australia's society women paid close attention to the vagaries of fashion, albeit at a distance from the salons of London or Paris. Most of these wealthy women employed dressmakers to make their costumes, ensuring originality and fit, but their less prosperous sisters were more likely to make their own, or to patronise one of the several drapers who advertised in the local press. J. Craven & Co. in Rundle Street described themselves as the 'Drapers of the Moment', promising 'charming styles' at 'very reasonable prices'. Competitors were Charles Birks ('the store noted for good value') and John Martins ('Best Value for the Money').[38] Prudent women no doubt compared all three.

The workplace

Such advertisements and fashion notes invariably shared column space with more prosaic household essentials – stoves, the Monarch Laundry ('Where Laundering is an Art'), furniture, tea and medicines. There was little doubt about the woman's sphere. In 1914 marriage remained the principal occupation for women in South Australia, despite slowly increasing rates of spinsterhood.[39] The economy was structured to ensure that this continued. Wages for women were generally set at half those of men, and even professional women seldom approached equality. The exception was women lawyers, but there were very few of them. Lawmakers remained blind to the hardship this caused women supporting families, preferring to protect the ideal of the male breadwinner and to preserve women's motivation to marry.

Nevertheless, increasing numbers of women were entering the paid workforce, both before and after marriage. The 'new' occupations like telephony and typewriting, that in the nineteenth century mainly employed men, were increasingly open to women, although debates about rates of pay continued. The various attempts to negotiate equal pay for equal work by typists in Victoria were widely reported in the South Australian press, prompting some local comment in support.[40] Others, like 'All Underpaid Youth', decried this movement of women into occupations previously reserved for men, fearing that women were forcing men's wages down:

> Employers can get women to work for 10/- per week for duties for which a man would want double that rate. Employers should be forced to pay wages irrespective of sex, but as things are now men hardly receive sufficient to keep themselves, much less wives. Women canvassers are also being employed by land and house agents.[41]

Here is a reference to another new occupation for women, agents selling houses and land, but the writer's main intent was to argue that women should be encouraged to remain in the home. 'In the writer's opinion', the article continued, 'mothers should teach their girls to cook and do housework, and he states that there are many positions available suitable for women, for which men cannot compete'.

'All Underpaid Youth' argued in vain. Although in 1914 both men and women continued to be employed as telephonists and typists (the occupation names were not then specifically gendered), this was changing rapidly. Advertisements like that placed by the Commonwealth Public Service Commissioner in March 1912 pointed the way to the future:

> The Commonwealth Public Service Commissioner is inciting applications from females between the ages of 16 and 25 for appointment as telephonists in the Postmaster-General's Department. Salary, minimum £39, maximum, £110 per annum.[42]

Women began to be employed as general clerks in business and in the public service too, but they were often employed on a temporary basis, on the assumption that their ultimate aim was marriage. Helen Jones pointed out that in 1914 there were only 10 female clerks employed on a permanent basis in the South Australian Government.[43]

Although South Australia always lagged behind Victoria in the scale of its industrial sector, manufacturing also employed many more women in the early twentieth century. In fact, the number of women employed in manufacturing more than doubled in the decade before the war.[44] The majority of these jobs were in the clothing and footwear trades, in workshops that varied in size from quite large establishments, employing 50 or more, to tiny concerns employing only a few workers. Many other women were employed as 'outworkers', or piece workers, supplying completed garments produced in their own homes. Piece work was notoriously difficult to regulate, although successive Inspectors of Factories made valiant efforts to do so, with the result that there was a great deal of exploitation. 'Sweating', as it was known, was believed to be widespread and was a recurring preoccupation of social reformers and concerned citizens in the decade before the war. Newspaper articles with headings like

'Shameful Sweating', or 'Sweated Women Workers' littered the press.[45] In November 1911 the Federated Clothing Trades Union highlighted several glaring instances of exploitation, alleging that one woman was paid just nine shillings for making three coats in a week, while another received just six shillings for three pairs of trousers. They demanded that the Minister for Industry in the Labor Government call together the Wages Board to 'take action at the earliest possible moment',[46] but from recurring comments in the press it seems likely that little was achieved.

1911 was not a good year for the Minister for Industry, James Phillips Wilson. In April he had been embarrassed to learn that waitresses in the Adelaide railway refreshment rooms were required to work between 80 and 82 hours per week for just 15 shillings in wages. To his credit, Wilson instituted an immediate enquiry, which confirmed the allegations. Describing the conditions under which the women worked as 'shocking', the Minister declared his intention to introduce legislation 'to prevent such scandalous conditions in the future'.[47] Faced with a hostile Legislative Council, however, the short-lived Labor ministry could do little to improve the operations of the Wages Board, especially as many workplaces continued to operate outside its jurisdiction. There were also continuing allegations of ineffective policing of wages and conditions, and of collusion with employers. In March 1914 the *Daily Herald* published a letter from a factory worker, under the headline 'Sweating in Adelaide: A factory worker's complaint'. 'Fairplay' complained that not only were 'Trousers hands' and shirt machinists required to make an unreasonable number of garments in a day, but that conditions in many workrooms were 'not fit for any girl to work in'. She asked:

> 'Why don't the inspectors go into the workrooms and talk to the girls instead of staying in the office or shop with the employer and calling each girl out to state her grievance in the presence of the employer? To voice any grievance in that case would mean a minute's notice to leave.[48]

Fairplay and others presented compelling arguments for reform, but it would be many decades before the right of women to earn a 'living wage' was recognised generally. In the meantime, many women struggled on, balanced precariously on the brink of abject poverty.

Women in more 'middle-class' occupations seldom continued to work after marriage. Even where they were permitted to continue (many were forced to resign), the 'double burden' of day job and domestic tasks proved too much, especially once children began to arrive. Some women, like Gertie Anderson, did manage to forge a new way, claiming both 'love and freedom', as Mackinnon has put it, but for most this was simply unattainable, even if they desired it. Most women in South Australia, new women or not, remained within the confines of the family. The modern family of 1914 was indeed beset by many tensions, pulled simultaneously both forward and back.

4

'Better protection and control' *Aboriginal people and the state in South Australia, 1901–1914*

MANDY PAUL

When the Australian colonies joined in 1901 to form the new Australian nation, and until 1911, South Australia included what is now the Northern Territory. The Constitution of the new nation gave the federal parliament the power to make laws with respect to 'the people of any race, other than the aboriginal race in any state', leaving the power to legislate in relation to Aboriginal people with the states.[1] This chapter outlines the significant changes in the administration of Aboriginal people in the period between 1901 and the outbreak of the First World War, highlighting the impact of racialised discourse in the relationship between Aboriginal people and the state in South Australia.

The new century

At the turn of the new century the Aboriginal inhabitants of the large central state of South Australia were administered, and conceptualised, as three groups. The first two were those in the remote tropical north, administered from Port Darwin, and those in Central Australia and what was known as the 'Far North' of South Australia, administered from Alice Springs and Port Augusta.[2] Government in these vast regions was represented by a network of Protectors, most of whom held this title, and duty, in addition to their main role as police officers, giving them the responsibility of both protecting and policing in what was still in many places a contested frontier. The work of the Protectors was supplemented by a network of ration depots located at stations on the Overland Telegraph Line, in towns and on pastoral stations.

The third group comprised those Aboriginal people in what was known euphemistically as 'the settled districts' of South Australia. In 1901 these survivors of the violence, disease and dislocation of colonisation were living in fringe camps around country towns, on pastoral stations and on missions.[3]

The largest mission was Point McLeay, in Ngarrindjeri country. The mission was established by the Aborigines' Friends' Association in 1859 at Raukkan, on the shores of Lake Alexandrina, and by the turn of the twentieth century there were about 200 people living there. About 100 people lived at Point Pierce, in Narungga country on Yorke Peninsula. Established in 1868, this mission was run by a local committee, the Yorke's Peninsula Aboriginal Mission Incorporated. In the far north-east of the state, Lutheran missionaries laboured in Dieri country at Killalpaninna, and reported that about 160 people were associated with the mission. In 1901 another Lutheran mission, Koonibba, was being established in Wirangu country on the west coast, and a short-lived mission at Manunka, near Swan Reach, was established by a Mr and Mrs Matthews. Poonindie, which had operated since 1850 in Barngala country near Port Lincoln, had closed in the mid-1890s, its residents dispersed, most to Point McLeay and Point Pierce.[4] As Peggy Brock has noted, these missions were established in the administrative vacuum left by the withdrawal of the state from financial and administrative responsibility for Aboriginal affairs in the 1860s.[5]

The Protector of Aborigines in 1901 was Edward Hamilton, who had been appointed in 1880 but had effectively held the office since 1873. The number of people under Hamilton's jurisdiction was difficult to estimate. A state census in 1901 calculated the number of 'Aborigines in the settled districts of South Australia, exclusive of the Northern Territory' at 3888.[6]

While the process of colonisation and attendant conflict over the occupation of land continued in northern and central Australia and the far north of South Australia, 'the land question' remained far from resolved even in the settled districts at the turn of the century. A system of Aboriginal reserves had been established in the 1840s as a form of recognition of Aboriginal proprietary rights to land, to be held in trust by the state to provide a source of income for the maintenance of those same people – and for a desired future in which Aboriginal people practiced cultivation in a form recognisable to those administering Crown land. Aboriginal people continued to apply for these and other blocks of land through a range of mechanisms.[7] In his 1901 report, Hamilton noted that 18 Aboriginal men had been 'given blocks of land under leases and permits' and that 'some of them are making progress towards earning their own living'.[8]

In 1897 Queensland had passed the Aboriginals Protection and Restriction of Sale of Opium Act. While there had been earlier Acts in Victoria and New South Wales, this Act became the model for new legislation in Western and South Australia to address what was described as 'the Aboriginal problem'. Following the passage of the Queensland Act, South Australia's premier Charles Kingston asked Charles Dashwood, Government Resident in Darwin, for a report on the 'condition of the Aborigines' in the Northern Territory. As in Queensland, the concerns reported focused on sexual relations between 'blacks', 'whites' and 'Asians' and the resulting children, the sexual abuse of Aboriginal women, and the effects of opium, alcohol and disease.[9]

The resulting Bill was referred to a Select Committee in 1899 after being passed in South Australia's Legislative Assembly. Drafted by Dashwood, it was intended primarily to meet the circumstances of the Northern Territory, but included all of South Australia in its jurisdiction. The employment provisions included in the Bill were the focus of significant opposition, particularly the requirements for written agreements (between Aboriginal employees and pastoralists) and the licensing of employers by Protectors. The other major stumbling block was the perception that legislation drafted with the frontier conditions of the Territory in mind was inappropriate for the settled areas of South Australia. The Select Committee rejected the Bill, but went on to recommend legislation that embodied the majority of its provisions, with the exception of the employment provisions.[10]

It was not only pastoralists and parliamentarians who opposed the employment provisions of the 1899 Bill. On 15 November 1899 the Hon. John Warren presented a petition to the Legislative Council signed by 29 residents of Point Pierce, objecting to this aspect of the Bill. The petition noted:

> The protection provided for in the Bill is, in our case, quite needless ... and, further we would point out that we, being electors for the House of Assembly object to the interference with our liberties if the Bill should become law ...[11]

In South Australia, Aboriginal men had been enfranchised to vote for the Legislative Assembly in 1856, and Aboriginal women in 1894. The work of Christine Finnimore and Pat Stretton demonstrated that this right had been exercised in 1896 by at least those at Point McLeay. The saving clause in the Australian Constitution, Section 41, designed to give women who had been enfranchised in some states the right to vote in federal elections, also had the effect of extending the rights of Aboriginal people in South Australia into the federal arena. Some of those at Point McLeay, at least, continued to vote in both state and federal elections well into the twentieth century. This right was contested and frequently hindered by bureaucratic practice.[12] However, if the franchise is one measure of citizenship, then it can be argued that Aboriginal people in South Australia held some form of citizenship in 1901 and took it with them into the Commonwealth. That citizenship would be compromised by debates and legislation premised on increasingly influential theories of race over the following decade and a half.

The reports of Protectors for the first decade and a half of the twentieth century followed a regular format, starting with reporting on population, calculations of which were based on a process of addition of births and subtraction of deaths recorded since the 1901 census, and concluding with the melancholy phrase 'excess of deaths' and a figure. The regular discussion of population figures, divided into two categories – 'Blacks' and 'Half-castes' – at once appeared to provide evidence for the prevalent theory that Aboriginal people were a 'doomed race' and simultaneously revealed something else. While the number of people in the first category, 'Blacks', was reported to be decreasing, the numbers of those in the second, 'Half-castes', was reported as increasing.

Racialised discourse was a dominant thread of public debate in Australia in the early twentieth century, a prism through which policy-makers constructed both how things were, and how they ought to be. Externally directed through the Immigration Restriction Act of 1901 (commonly referred to as the White Australia Policy), within Australia the categorisation of Aboriginal people into groups according to theories of race was to have a major impact on the lives of those people so defined, their families and their communities. Aboriginal people were increasingly described and defined in terms of fractions of race, and those of mixed descent defined as a problem. As Rob Foster suggested, 'By the turn of the century the very idea of "half-castes" began to take on connotations of immorality, and interracial relationships were increasingly regarded as unnatural'.[13] This represented a distinct shift. In the colonial period in South Australia, for example, grants of land were made to Aboriginal women who married non-Aboriginal men, a practice instituted in 1848 as an inducement both to marriage and a particular land use (cultivation). By the turn of the century this practice was being re-thought, as such marriages were rendered problematic by changing concerns on the part of those administering Aboriginal people.[14]

In his 1905 report, Protector Hamilton welcomed the Premier's announcement of his government's intention to legislate 'for the protection of Aborigines', concluding that 'the necessity for additional legislation for the better control and management of the aborigines has for some time been felt and admitted'. Hamilton continued, 'The question of how to manage a new race of educated half-castes and quadroons, who are increasing in number, requires serious consideration'.[15] In 1907 Hamilton again mentioned the 'much needed' legislation, arguing that South Australia was the only state still without an Aborigines Act. He referred back to the recommendations of the 1899 Select

Committee and noted that a draft Bill had been in preparation for some time.[16]

In early 1908 the long-serving Hamilton retired and William Garnet South was appointed Protector. South had been a mounted constable in Alice Springs, and from 1898 he had been stationed in Adelaide.[17] In his first report as Protector he wrote:

> A Bill for an Act for the better protection and control of the aborigines, prepared by Mr. Hamilton and myself, has already been sent along, and I trust it will this session of Parliament become law. In my opinion separate Acts are required for South Australia and the Northern Territory, as in South Australia proper the chief problem is the half-caste, who is yearly increasing.[18]

He went on to support his point by reciting the respective numbers of 'half-castes' and 'blacks' at Point Pearce and Point McLeay.

> From this it will be seen that the aboriginal problem is rapidly assuming a different aspect than it bore some years ago. In comparatively a few years the old type of native will probably have died out and be replaced by a race of educated half-castes, with a sprinkling of blacks.[19]

South pursued solutions to this perceived problem more aggressively than his predecessor. By the following year he was able to inform the government that the State Children's Department was now willing to take charge of 'half-caste' children – and stated that it was his intention to have 'all wandering and half-caste children' committed to the care of the Council, where they would 'be educated and trained to useful trades' and 'prevented from acquiring the habits and customs of

This image appeared in the report of the Protector of Aborigines for 1911. It shows Paddy and Willie Robinson, who were removed from their family. [History SA, SAGPC GN 01177]

the aborigines'.[20] Cameron Raynes suggests that South's career in the police force may have assisted him in obtaining a list from the Commissioner of Police of 766 'half-castes' in the state, presumably to be used as the basis for his campaign.[21]

Among the children pictured in South's 1911 report were Willie and Paddy Robinson, aged nine and seven respectively. They had appeared on the 'List of Half Caste Aborigines in South Australia', and had been removed from their family in Renmark and committed to the Industrial School at Edwardstown.[22] The children's mother wrote to South: 'this note is an appeal to you to endeavor to regain possession of my children which was taken from me under false pretenses ... I can assure you they were never neglected ...'. The editor of the *Renmark Pioneer* wondered at the legality of the practice: 'I cannot conceive that it was ever the intention of the legislature that native lads should be torn from their parents without their consent'.[23]

South Australia legislates

In Darwin, Charles Herbert, successor to Dashwood as Government Resident, was also agitating for legislation. A Bill, first discussed in the South Australian Parliament in late 1908, was finally passed in early December 1910, only three weeks before the Northern Territory was relinquished to the control of the Commonwealth. The Act established a Northern Territory Aboriginals Department, headed up by a Chief Protector, and made the Chief Protector the legal guardian of every 'aboriginal and every half-caste child' under 18 years of age. Other major provisions concerned the declaration of reserves, other institutions and prohibited areas; the regulation of employment, including the requirement that employers of 'any aboriginal or any female half-caste' be licensed; and restrictions on the use of firearms by Aboriginal people. The Act also included a range of 'protective' provisions designed to restrict sexual relations between Aboriginal people and non-Aboriginal people, including the prohibition of the marriage of 'a female aboriginal with any person other than an aboriginal' without written permission from a Protector, and prohibitions on entering the camps of 'aboriginals or female half-castes'.[24]

The South Australian Bill was introduced in August 1910, with the new Labor Premier, John Verran, noting that the aim was 'to legislate not only for the protection and care of those people, but also for their control'.[25] The Bill lapsed, was re-introduced

ANNO SECUNDO

GEORGII V REGIS.

A.D. 1911.

****

No. 1048.

An Act to make provision for the better Protection and Control of the Aboriginal and Half-caste Inhabitants of the State of South Australia.

[*Assented to, December 7th, 1911.*]

BE it Enacted by the Governor of the State of South Australia, with the advice and consent of the Parliament thereof, as follows:

1. This Act may be cited as "The Aborigines Act, 1911." Short title.

2. The Ordinance No. 12 of 1844, being an Ordinance to provide for the protection, maintenance, and up-bringing of orphans and other destitute children of the aborigines, is hereby repealed: Provided that such repeal shall not alter the effect of the doing or omission of any thing before the passing of this Act, and shall not affect any right granted, obligation imposed, liability incurred, or any offence committed by, under, or against the said Ordinance, or any proceedings commenced before or after the passing of this Act with respect to any of such matters or things. Repeal.

Interpretation.

3. In this Act, unless inconsistent with the context or subject matter— Definitions.

"Aboriginal institution" means and includes any mission station, reformatory, orphanage, school, home, reserve, or other institution for the benefit, care, or protection of the aboriginal or half-caste inhabitants of the State: W.A., 14, 1905, s. 2.

A—1048 "Chief

The restrictive provisions of the Aborigines Act of 1911 were to endure for half a century.

in August 1911 and finally assented to in December 1911. Its subtitle was 'An Act to make provision for the Better Protection and Control of the Aboriginal and Half-caste Inhabitants of the State of South Australia'. The Act established an Aborigines Department, charged with 'the duty of controlling and promoting the welfare of the aboriginals', at its head a Chief Protector. Section 4 defined as 'aboriginal' any 'aboriginal native of Australia', any 'half-caste' (a person who has an aboriginal parent or grandparent) who is husband or wife of, or who 'habitually lives or associates with', 'aboriginal natives', or any 'half-caste child whose age does not apparently exceed sixteen years'. Section 10 (1) made the Chief Protector legal guardian of 'every aboriginal and every half-caste child, notwithstanding that any such child has a parent or other relative living, until such child attains the age of twenty-one years, except whilst such child is a State child'.

The Act also gave the Chief Protector sweeping powers to control the movement and residence of Aboriginal people. This included section 17 (1), which related to the power to cause 'any aboriginal or half-caste' to be kept in or removed to a reserve or institution. Section 31 enabled a Protector to order Aboriginal people to remove their camps from any town or municipality, and Section 32 gave the governor the power to declare areas prohibited to Aboriginal people. The Act also provided for the allocation to Aboriginal people of blocks of land 'not exceeding one hundred and sixty acres'.

In his second reading speech, Chief Secretary the Hon. Frederick Wallis, Member of the Legislative Council, explained the history of the Bill. He noted that similar legislation had been contemplated for some years, beginning with the 1899 Bill, that another Bill was drafted by Protector Hamilton in 1905, and then another by Governor Hunt was mostly adopted in the form of the Act relating to Northern Territory Aborigines the previous year. He went on to note that the Bill now being presented had been introduced at the same time as the Northern Territory Bill, and contained the same provisions with certain omissions, but did not get beyond its second reading.[26] He outlined the main clauses of the Bill, including an addition to the provisions of the Northern Territory Bill, suggested by Protector South, making it an offence 'for any female aborigine or half-caste to be found in male attire in the company of a male person who was not an aborigine or half-caste'.[27] This was eventually section 34 of the Act. Wallis also noted the provisions omitted 'as it was considered they were not required for the aborigines and half-castes of South Australia':

> Prohibition of intermarriage between aborigines and other persons, except with the permission of a protector; prohibition of employment of aborigines except by licensed persons; restrictions upon the possession and use of firearms by aborigines; and prohibition of entering the camps of aborigines or female half-castes.[28]

He concluded by reminding members that the Bill was largely based on the Acts, now in force for some time, in Queensland and Western Australia.

A number of members who spoke on the Bill articulated a shared logic that 'something should be done' for the original inhabitants of the state who had lost their land and livelihood. As the Hon. John Warren put it, 'a reason why South Australians should strive for the welfare of the aborigines was they had occupied the country that was formerly the happy hunting ground of the tribes'.[29]

It was generally observed, and accepted, by those speaking on the Bill that 'blacks' were 'dying out', and that the question which needed to be addressed was 'the half-caste problem'.[30] The Hon. John James Duncan noted that 'the mixed race numbered about one-fourth of the aboriginal inhabitants of the State', that 'white blood, being the stronger must in the end prevail'; and that:

> it is evident that the ultimate end of the Australian aborigine is to be merged into the general population; consequently the sooner they are physically and morally improved, the better for the white race.[31]

Removal of 'half-caste' children was the method advocated to achieve this, a method that was also, it was argued, 'best for the children'.[32]

While a number of speakers acknowledged that the mothers of these children would object to having their children removed, only one, Hermann Homburg – representing the district of Murray – argued against the Protector having the power to separate children from their mothers 'simply because there was colour in the skin of their children'.[33] One amendment made in committee was the raising of the age to which the Chief Protector was guardian of Aboriginal children from 18 to 21 years.[34]

One argument relating to land is worth noting. As the Hon. John Lewis put it, 'white people owed the aborigines a great deal. They had taken away their country and given them very little in return; and that was no fault of the natives'.[35] Lewis was not alone in noting that the system of reserves of land made for Aboriginal people in the nineteenth century had not been honoured, that much of it had been sold and the funds directed into general revenue.[36] A new clause was added to the Bill in the

House of Assembly enabling the Protector to purchase land to be occupied by Aboriginal people. The aim was to 'save the half-castes' through separation and cultivation: they would, 'if placed apart on suitable blocks of land ... cultivate the soil profitably to themselves and to the State'.[37] When returned to the Legislative Council, the clause was amended to enable the Protector to 'allot to any aboriginal a block not exceeding 160 acres any Crown lands available for settlement, or may purchase land for such occupation'. This brought across into the legislation a clause in the Crown Lands Act of 1903.[38] This debate, and the provision in the Act, reveals both the continued centrality of 'the land question' some 85 years after official settlement, as well as the continuing belief in a relationship between cultivation and civilisation.

The parliamentary debate framed the Bill as a positive intervention, a move to 'do something for' the original inhabitants of the state. The only comment on the powers of the new role of Chief Protector was by the Hon. John James Duncan, who spoke in support, stating that the 'additional powers were urgently required to enable him to cope with and regulate all matters relating to the natives'.[39]

Extending state control

Over a decade after it was first proposed, South Australia now had an Aborigines Act. Protector South ascended to the new role of Chief Protector. The thrust of the new Act was summarised in the *Daily Herald* in March of the following year: 'the idea of the Act is to give the State better control over the aborigines, and provide for placing natives in reserves'.[40] The lack of many of the protective provisions included in the Northern Territory Act reflected that despite the South Australian Act's subtitle, the government was moving to exercise control rather than protection. Its effect was to set the stage for a regime of control over the lives of Aboriginal people, based on categories of race, that was to last half a century.

Barely three months after the Act came into force, its provisions were used to remove Aboriginal people from Adelaide. Chief Protector South reported:

> The camps which existed about the city have been broken up and the old, disreputable natives transferred to Point McLeay, where they are well-provided for by the department, and are much better off and happier than while begging and drinking about the city.[41]

In his report for 1912, South noted that children removed from 'the aborigines' camps' were 'doing well' under the control of the State Children's Department, and argued that 'the good work of rescue should be vigorously continued'. But his main focus following the passage of the Act was to argue for 'a complete change of the control of the aborigines'. South argued that 'the divided control of the aborigines, between the Department and the Mission, is most unsatisfactory', and went on to claim that those living at Point Pierce and Point McLeay were 'constantly asking me to do what I can to induce the Government to take over the control of these stations and work them as industrial institutions for the able-bodied ones and as homes for the old and infirm'.[42]

South explained that his main desire in advocating government takeover of the missions was not to save taxpayers money, but rather the wish to raise those living there 'from the idle, thriftless habits of the black to the level of the white race'. He continued:

> This I regard as most important, as in the settled districts the blacks are rapidly dying out and being replaced by a race of half-castes, quadroons, and octoroons, who in turn must inevitably be merged in the general population.[43]

On 6 November 1912, only a few months after South's report was tabled in Parliament, William Angus, professor of agriculture and Member for Victoria and Albert, proposed a Royal Commission into the management of Aboriginal institutions. His proposal had two main arguments: firstly, that the missions (Point McLeay particularly) were not succeeding in educating and training those living there for 'the life ahead of them', who were instead 'living in idleness'. He stated that this was not through the fault of those running the mission, but rather because they did not have the means at their disposal and that 'they were bearing a burden that the state should bear'. Secondly, it was the 'shame of the state' that 'so many quadroon and half-caste children were allowed to run about and grow up as savages'.[44] The following week Angus noted that 'there is a good deal of opposition raised by sentimental people to any proposal to take the children from their mothers. But the interests of the state and of the children themselves have to be considered'.[45] In December 1912 a Royal Commission was established by the South Australian Parliament. Its terms of reference were:

> to inquire into and report upon the control, organisation, and management of the institutions in this State set aside for the benefit of the aborigines, and generally upon the whole question of the South Australian aborigines ...[46]

Angus was appointed chair. The initial work of the Commission, detailed in a progress report to parliament in October 1913, concerned itself with the work of the Aborigines Department and Point McLeay and Point Pierce Missions (run by the Aborigines' Friends Association and the Yorke's Peninsula Aboriginal Mission Incorporated respectively). The Royal Commission took evidence between February and July 1913, in Queensland and New South Wales, as well as in Adelaide, Point McLeay, Point Pierce and Moonta.

The Commission was of the opinion that the work of Point McLeay Mission was 'not a success'. Having outlined its dependence on government grants, the report stated that the Mission was 'languishing', that 'the aborigines and half-castes are being reared for the most part in idleness, and instead of the natives being trained to useful work, they have, to a great extent, become dependent on charity'. In conclusion, the Commission reported 'we are strongly convinced that under more direct Government control much better results could easily be secured'.[47] While more positive about Point Pierce, which the Commission found was 'so well managed' that it was self-supporting, it likewise concluded that 'more use might be made of the natives in farming operations' even at the expense of financial results.[48]

The focus of questioning of Aboriginal people called as witnesses was control of the missions, employment, and the question of establishing Aboriginal people on blocks of land. When Alfred Hughes, of Point Pierce, was asked the source of his discontent, he replied bluntly 'it is the land question; we want to get on the land'.[49] This was a consistent theme among Aboriginal witnesses appearing before the Commission. They argued for the abolition of the system of (white) farmers working mission land, and for Aboriginal people to be put on blocks with some government help to get established.

A number of Aboriginal witnesses expressed concern that,

as Tom Adams, at Point Pierce, put it, 'some provision be made for the younger generation'.[50] While some witnesses agreed that providing industrial training for young people would be a good idea and some agreed, when pressed, that children should be sent away for this purpose if necessary, others pointed out that parents would never agree to such a course – as Matthew Kropinyeri, from Point McLeay, said:

> In regard to the taking of our children in hand by the State to learn trades, &c, our people would gladly embrace the opportunity of betterment for our children; but to be subjected to complete alienation from our children is to say the least an unequalled act of injustice, and no parent worthy of the name would either yield to or urge such a measure.[51]

The Commission, on the other hand, outlined the rationale for its proposed reforms, arguing that:

> There is no doubt that in the early days, and for many years afterwards, it was necessary for the Government to protect the native inhabitants; but with the gradual disappearance of the full-blood blacks, the mingling of the black and white races, and the great increase in the number of half-castes and quadroons, the problem is now one of assisting and training the native so that he may become a useful member of the community, dependent not upon charity but upon his own efforts.[52]

This reasoning was consistent with, and an extension of, the arguments put in the South Australian Parliament for the Aborigines Act. It is also, as Charles Rowley pointed out in his classic work, an early expression of the ideas that were to underpin the later policy of Assimilation.[53]

The progress report contained 26 recommendations. Key among them was that the Mission Stations at Point Pierce and Point McLeay be taken over by the government, to be controlled by the Aborigines Department, and that the Department be controlled by a board. It was also recommended that the system of share-farming at Point Pierce be phased out and that as an experiment 'one or two' of the 'best trained' men from each mission be settled on small blocks. The Commission made a number of recommendations based on those it termed 'half-castes', notably that that the able-bodied 'should not be dependent on the charity of the Government' and should be compelled to go into 'outside employment wherever possible', and that training for boys (in trades and farm work) and girls (in domestic work) should be compulsory in order to fit them for such employment. Significantly, recommendation 17 read: 'That it is desirable to separate as much as possible the full-bloods from the half-caste natives, each living in a separate community'. The Commission also recommended the removal of children be encouraged and extended.[54]

The second phase of the work of the Royal Commission was carried out between January and July 1914, investigating conditions at the Lutheran-run Koonibba and Killalpaninna Missions, in the state's west and north. The Commission was impressed by the management and conditions at Koonibba, noting that it was the only place in South Australia where 'births of Aborigines are in excess of the deaths'. Commissioners were less impressed with Killalpaninna, noting that 'the aboriginals in the Far North are gradually dying out'. They also concluded that 'it is the duty of the Government to acquire possession of [Koonibba and Killalpaninna] and assume direct responsibility for the well-being of the blacks, as has been done at Point McLeay and Point Pierce'. This formed the basis of the first of the Commission's two final recommendations; the other was to make provision for notification of cases of venereal disease.[55]

Conclusion

The period between 1901 and 1914 saw a number of significant shifts in the relationship between Aboriginal people and the state in South Australia. The relinquishing of the Northern Territory to the new Commonwealth was paralleled by a shift in discourse and practice in relation to Aboriginal people in settled South Australia. The period under discussion saw the rise of the categorisation of people according to theories of race. As the 'doomed race' theory was modified in the face of dis-aggregated population figures, the focus shifted from protection to control. Perceived as frontier concerns, the measures designed to control sexual violence and sexual relationships between Aboriginal people and non-Aboriginal people were transmuted in the legislation and practice relating to South Australia. After an absence of half a century, the state stepped back in to regulate the lives of Aboriginal people, implementing a race-based regime of control and segregation.

The Aborigines Act of 1911 gave the state the power to control the movement of Aboriginal people and to segregate them from the wider community. The implementation of recommendations of the Royal Commission of 1913 and 1914 also saw the state gain control of Point Pierce (in 1915), Point McLeay (1916) and Killalpaninna (1919).[56] Those Aboriginal people defined as 'half-castes' were to find themselves the focus of government control. When calling in 1912 for the Royal Commission, William Angus had argued that the removal of children was in 'the interests of the state and of the children themselves'.[57] This accorded with Chief Protector South's views, and, empowered by the new legislative regime, his department intensified the removal of children from their families and communities. The devastating impacts of this practice on individuals, families and communities continue to be felt more than a century later.

During the hearings of the Royal Commission at Point Pierce in July 1913, Joe Edwards, '(aboriginal)', was called and examined. He argued, 'we have grown beyond the mission life', to which the Chairman, William Angus, responded:

> You have the whole Commonwealth of Australia open to you just the same as other responsible citizens, and if you have gone beyond being helped by the station then you should go out into the world and help yourself.[58]

By 1914, however, Aboriginal people in South Australia can be seen as having a contingent, or compromised, citizenship. Although Aboriginal people had the right to vote in both state and federal elections, it was a right constrained by administrative practice. And the wider citizenship of Aboriginal people was severely compromised by the powers of control vested in the Chief Protector and his department under the provisions of the Aborigines Act. Joe Edwards could not 'go out into the world' 'just the same as other responsible citizens'; his movements were subject to regulation by the Chief Protector of Aborigines. An understanding of the rise of racialised discourse and its implementation as policy in the period under discussion raises new questions about the motivations behind, and meanings of, the significant rate of enlistment of Aboriginal men from South Australia during the First World War.

5

'Of Course you have to take the Rough with the Smooth'
South Australia's British farm apprenticeship scheme

ELSPETH GRANT

In July 1914, 42 boys emigrated from Britain after signing up for the new farm apprenticeships on offer in South Australia. They disembarked at Outer Harbor on 11 July 1914, caught the train to Adelaide Station and walked down North Terrace to the Exhibition Building. Here they spent their first night in their new land before completing the journeys to their new homes across the state. These young immigrants were not to know that before a month had passed the First World War would start.

This chapter will explore what this farm apprenticeship scheme for British boys tells us about agriculture in South Australia on the eve of the First World War, especially with regard to labour and the 'Great Eastern' drought.[1] The circumstances that necessitated such a scheme will be investigated, followed by an exploration of the conditions faced by both the apprentices and their host farmers. It will show that the years immediately preceding the First World War were not only a time of overt optimism but also of grave misfortune for South Australia's agricultural industry.

Youth migration and agriculture

South Australian agriculture and migration resumed their

British farm apprentices who disembarked from the SS *Orsova* on 11 July 1914, in the Jubilee Oval grandstand adjacent to the Exhibition Building, Adelaide.[2] [History SA, SAGPC GN 01102]

duet in the 1910s, a song that had been sung on and off from the outset of European settlement. Assisted passages for the 'owners of labour' were a vital feature of the Wakefield Plan that underpinned the establishment of the colony, and the state's 1911 and 1913 Immigration Acts replaced legislation allowing for subsidised emigration from the last major expansion of colonisation, between 1869 and 1879.[3] This was the first boom in immigration since Federation in 1901 and several programs facilitating unaccompanied child and youth migration from Britain to Australia were initiated across the new nation in this period. Such programs went on to become the subject of formal apologies by the governments of both nations in recent years.[4]

South Australia's British farm apprenticeship scheme was

put into effect shortly after the better-known Dreadnought Trust was established at Scheyville, New South Wales, and Kingsley Fairbridge founded his long-lived movement at Pinjarra in Western Australia.[5] For reasons summarised below, South Australia's first batch of farm apprentices did not arrive until June 1913. This came just after what was to prove the high-water mark of assisted migration prior to the Second World War, as Eric Richards has pointed out: 'Immigration from Britain had already slackened after the great peak of 1912, and was certainly subsiding well before the war was declared in August 1914'.[6]

Consistent with most other Australian assisted migration schemes aimed at British males in the early to mid-twentieth century, South Australia's centred on agriculture.[7] The South Australian government adopted a farm apprenticeship model that imperialist Thomas Sedgwick had previously trialled on a smaller scale in New Zealand and Canada.[8] It largely outsourced the government's financial commitment (beyond the scheme's subsidised passages and administration) to the state's farmers, rather than requiring investment in a Scheyville- or Pinjarra-style training farm that would educate young migrants before they sought employment.[9] There were various factors that ultimately limited the government's control over the apprentices' backgrounds but, like other states and dominions playing in the imperial migration arena, South Australia ideally sought 'the good yeoman stock of Britain'.[10]

Demand for agricultural labour

Setting aside the 'imperial rhetoric' associated with British child and youth migration, the primary aim of the government's farm apprenticeship scheme was clearly to boost the state's rural labour force by having these young immigrants settle in the countryside.[11] The years Richards periodised as 'the slow awakening' for migration in Australia (1900–1914) coincide with what Michael Williams characterised as a period of 'over-confidence', 'recklessness' and 'unthinking expansion' into what were previously considered uncultivable areas in South Australia.[12] Towards the epoch of this ebullience, Governor Sir Day Hort Bosanquet declared that the 'continuance of prosperity and expansion of South Australian agricultural industries was … practically assured'.[13] Overt optimism is also evident in the farm apprentice recruitment brochure, which contains a fold-out map of South Australia stating:

> AGRICULTURAL LANDS – Large Areas are in course of Survey and will be offered as Surveys are completed. About 3,500,000 Acres will be offered during the next few years. IRRIGATION AND RECLAMATION – Areas are being prepared for offer in the Valley of the River Murray. PASTORAL LANDS – Large Areas available for occupation.[14]

This expansion also impacted upon the agricultural areas of the state already relatively well-established, as farmer Alexander Hamilton succinctly summarised at a Blyth Agricultural Bureau meeting in 1913: 'Owing largely to closer settlement, and the quantity of new land being brought under cultivation … there was a growing scarcity of labor [*sic*]'.[15] Although mechanisation helped, South Australia's increasingly inadequate agricultural labour force appeared to require urgent intervention for the 'huge hopefulness' – which Michelle Hetherington asserts was typical of this era across Australia – to be realised.[16]

John Verran's Labor and Archibald Peake's Liberal Union governments attempted to tackle the agricultural labour shortage in three main ways: encouraging South Australian farmers to sponsor adult British migrants, training South Australian boys at a farm school, and, finally, conflating both ideas by encouraging farmers to take on British boys as apprentices. 'An Act to encourage Immigration' was assented to in 1911, which enabled Verran's government to (re)establish a system by which South Australian farmers could sponsor the emigration of British men. Supply issues aside, demand was limited.[17] This was partly due not only to the dual deterrents of a sizeable fee and no obligation on the part of the employee to remain with his sponsor, but also because of a common assumption that adult migrants came with fixed ideas and non-transferable skills.[18] For example, farmer Archibald Koch reported to the Lameroo Agricultural Bureau:

> With carpenters and other tradesmen their work is the same, whether they are engaged in Australia or any other part of the world. When once the technical part is mastered it is only slightly altered to work with local conditions. An English farm hand is, however, faced with an altogether different problem. He finds that his several years of farm life in England will not stand him in much stead. He may be able to drive a wagon team, or harness horses, but as far as implements are concerned, he would certainly have to start at the bottom of the ladder and work his way up.[19]

After Peake resumed office in February 1912 he removed the sponsorship fee but landowners were still loathe to invest in adult migrant workers; as one Agricultural Bureau reported, 'the general opinion was that newcomers as a rule were not worth current rates of wages until they had at least served a term under local conditions'.[20] He also took the farmers' feedback regarding the fixed abilities of these adults on board and opened a training farm for South Australian boys at North Booborowie (approximately 200 kilometres north of Adelaide). However, only ten boys from Adelaide signed up and by July the Minister of Agriculture stated that he was 'rather disappointed that the farm school had not been taken greater advantage of'.[21] Hence by mid-1912 the government instead turned to youth migration, embracing Sedgwick's farm apprenticeship model for British boys aged 15 to 19 years.

The system required no upfront payment by the farmer and obliged the apprentice to stay with his master for the duration of his contract. It also provided the employers with malleable employees; the government advised that:

> this scheme is superior in many respects to adult immigration. The boys would have nothing to unlearn, and would arrive at an age when they would be able to adapt themselves to South Australian conditions.[22]

Farmers, including Hamilton, agreed: 'The proposal to import lads from England, and train them specifically for farm work, was to his mind a good one. Youths naturally adapted themselves more quickly to the conditions of the country'.[23] Some ambiguity remained, however, about whether experience in farming prior to emigration was a help or a hindrance, and South Australia's agent-general in Britain sourced 22 boys from the Boy Scouts' Buckhurst Place Farm School and the Royal Philanthropic Society's Farm School in Sussex, England, and the Kibble Farm School in Paisley, Scotland (despite the two latter establishments being reformatories).[24] The Labor opposition voiced a more cynical evaluation of the motives behind recruiting young migrants: 'Behind the scheme was the desire of the farming community to get labor [*sic*] at a cheap rate'.[25]

Thomas Brennand's report to the Koppio Agricultural Bureau suggests there may have been some truth in this:

> The growing scarcity of experienced and reliable farm hands, *together with the high rate of wages demanded by farm laborers,*[*sic*] is evidently becoming a problem to the farming community who cultivate large areas and have to employ them.[26]

The farm apprentices arrive

Suitable applicants for South Australia's British farm apprenticeship scheme were sought in Britain until recruitment halted with the outbreak of war. Between June 1913 and July 1914, 171 migrants arrived to assume one- to three-year apprenticeships on farms from Penong in the far west, through to Port MacDonnell in the lower south-east.[27] Many of the farmers who took on an apprentice were well-established and will be familiar to historians of rural and regional South Australia (to list a few in addition to those featured in this chapter: Stuckey of Rendelsham, Knappstein of Clare, Wyllie of Renmark, and Telfer of Sheringa).[28] Others were relatively new to farming and/or small operators under the Closer Settlement movement. There is a correlation between agricultural bureau members and farmers who took on an apprentice, reflecting the role that the bureaux played in endorsing and publicising the scheme and partly explaining the clustering of apprentices in some areas, such as the mid-north and lower Flinders Ranges.[29] The Immigration Officer sought an assessment of each potential employer from the local police and other trusted authority figures in the district. The reports addressed the following points:

1. The farmer's reputation as regards treatment of employés.
2. Is he a married man and does he reside with his family on the land?
3. Is he a man of temperate habits and of good moral character?
4. Whether in your officer's opinion the boy will have an opportunity of gaining good all-round experience in farming operations.
5. Whether the farmer is sufficiently established to offer *permanent* employment.
6. Whether accommodation provided for employés is satisfactory.[30]

Unfortunately, it does not appear that any of the confidential responses were archived and so have been lost to the historical record. Instead, glimpses of the reality of agriculture in South Australia at this time can be discerned amongst the propaganda in the aforementioned brochure circulated in Britain to encourage boys to apply for an apprenticeship. South Australia was branded on the front cover as the 'wheat and garden state', reflecting the fact that approximately 89 per cent of South Australia's arable land was used for growing wheat at this time.[31] This was also reflected in the type of work undertaken by most apprentices; only some boys were placed on properties that focussed on fruit growing and dairying, while pastoralists were not eligible to apply.[32] The brochure did not gild the lily when describing the nature of farm labour:

> The work will, of course, be hard, dull, and monotonous at times, and on some days the hours will be long, and owing to farms in South Australia being, as a rule, scattered and distant from

> towns, the boy may at first experience a feeling of loneliness ... Although the food and prospects are good, only willing hard workers succeed.[33]

In terms of duties, 'the work [would] include milking, stone-picking, ploughing, carting water, clearing and burning scrub, fencing, chaff-cutting, attending to stock and poultry, trapping rabbits, chopping wood, odd jobs, and general farm work'.[34] The brochure contained 12 photographs illustrating farming in South Australia, with the annual wheat harvest dominating; they show that the industry was clearly still reliant on both man- and horse-power.[35] The rapid expansion of agricultural land was also portrayed: an image of 'Virgin Mallee Land' was juxtaposed with photographs of productive cleared properties.[36] The lone 'Grape-picker at Work in a Vineyard near Adelaide' was at odds with both the type of work undertaken by, and distant placement of, most apprentices.[37]

Many positive quotes from letters to the Immigration Officer by boys who arrived in the first shipment were used in the recruitment brochure, for example:

> I would much rather be here than in the old country.
>
> I can see I am better off than when I was in England.
>
> There is nothing to stop me from getting on and becoming a farmer within a few years.
>
> I try to learn all I can in farming, as I hope, in three or four years, to try share farming.[38]

Early media reports relying on the government as their source were also glowing. The Adelaide press published an upbeat letter to the Immigration Officer by another of the inaugural participants, which advised that the apprentice had

'A Complete Harvester – Bagging the Grain', one of many images in the farm apprenticeship recruitment brochure showing limited mechanisation.[39] [History SA, SAGPC GN 11487]

already been offered a share in his host's farm. The boy was also fulfilling the scheme's aim of boosting the rural population and labour force by planning to nominate the girlfriend he left behind in England to join him as soon as practicable – she could initially continue with domestic service work, as was her current occupation in England, and presumably they would then marry and procreate once the apprentice was earning a full wage.[40]

However, there is also a considerable volume of extant records that give a more balanced account of the experiences of the apprentices and their hosts. State Records of South Australia holds a file for each and every farm apprentice, with most containing enlightening correspondence as well as an application form, apprenticeship agreement, and pay and procurement paperwork.[41] The boys were encouraged to correspond with the Immigration Officer, Edgar Field, and most were literate and articulate.[42] These archives are particularly significant as they provide first-hand testimony, and are also unusual as they give a 'voice' to child and youth migrants about the program under which they migrated.[43] Similarly, they give a voice to agricultural labourers, whose perspective is often omitted from rural and regional histories due to a farmhand's relative under-representation in formal records, high itinerancy and relatively low standing in society. It is through these files that we can discover that the author of the aforementioned anonymous letter published in the press was Frederick Ward, a former assistant patternmaker from London, initially apprenticed under Heinrich (Henry) Wegner at Appila in the mid-north and then by George White and Ruth Crook in the Murray Mallee. It was not relayed to or reported by the media that his 'intended' had already married someone else by the time he forwarded her passage money.[44] It is from another of Ward's letters that this chapter takes its name.[45]

Due to the popularity of genealogy, these records are now being accessed by family historians related to the farm apprentices.[46] In general, these primary sources remain underutilised for broader research, yet they disclose a good deal about the state of affairs in South Australia on the eve of the First World War, including agriculture at farm, district and state-wide levels.

Drought hits

Collectively, the farm apprentices' files tell the story of the Great Eastern Drought, which took hold across several Australian states in mid-1914. Rebecca Jones calls it the 'forgotten drought, overshadowed by the longevity of its predecessor, the

Damming the River Murray at Waikerie, 1914 – such were the conditions faced by 11 apprentices situated along the river. [History SA, SAGPC GN 09242]

federation drought' and explains that, using modern parlance, 'meteorologists now identify 1914–1915 as a strong "El Nino" event'.[47] The drought was acute: while it only lasted about 13 months (from approximately April 1914 to May 1915), it was exceptionally severe. It left an enduring mark on quantitative data concerning South Australian agriculture and usually stands out as a one-year chasm on column graphs.[48] The immigration records provide a qualitative context regarding the impact of the drought on people, stock and the land.

Applications for farm apprentices by farmers dried up as the drought progressed. The outbreak of war stopped further shipments of British farm apprentices arriving but there was still the problem of what to do with those who had already arrived, some as late as July 1914.[49] Boy Scout George Langborne, from the Isle of Wight, had been apprenticed by Samuel Cozens at Black Rock in 1913. Immigration Officer Field wrote to him in October 1914 that:

> It is extremely unfortunate for you and other boys who have come from England that you should this year encounter the worst drought on record, but you must keep a stiff upper lip, and brave hardships if necessary, as good times are ahead, and I am sure that you will eventually be successful.[50]

Shortly after this, Field became busy administering the Drought Relief Act of 1914 but still managed to continue responding to letters from the farm apprentices and their hosts.[51] Charlie Whitehead was one of a small number of boys transferred from his initial placement (at Georgetown) to a government-run farm (at nearby Hallett) following the failure of the 1914 harvest.[52] By March 1915 Field advised Whitehead that 'this drought has altered the whole condition of affairs in South Australia, and therefore it is impossible for us to fully carry out the scheme for placing the lads on farms in the way it was intended'.[53] It seemed that a 'stiff upper lip' was not going to suffice after all.[54]

'You are fortunate to be employed in the South East at present, as the boys in the North are having a bad time on account of the Drought,' Field divulged to an apprentice working at Naracoorte in November 1914.[55] As mentioned above, there was a relatively large number of apprentices placed in the state's mid-north and the lower Flinders Ranges. Farmer Richard Dawson Hanna, of Port Germein, was reading the writing on the wall by April 1914: 'the season here is not opening too favourably and should it prove to be only a fair one I will have to cut and cart wood to Port Pirie'.[56] Six months later Hanna joined the many farmers from this region seeking to be relieved of responsibility for their apprentices. Field sought direction from the Commissioner of Crown Lands and Immigration and a few farmers were told to honour their apprenticeship agreements as 'perhaps we will be blessed with a good rain shortly':

> Apprenticeship has the advantage of securing the farmer when labor [sic] is scarce and must of course carry the obligation to employ when times are bad. Whilst the present crop may be a failure that fact does not prove that you are unable to pay the boy's wages ... one would expect farmers in a good district like Gulnare to be in a position to withstand the very occasional set back of a drought.[57]

On the other hand, many masters, including Hanna, were permitted to suspend the agreement in the hope they would at least continue to accommodate the young migrants

> The Commissioner now directs me to say that under the very exceptional circumstance caused by the unprecedented Drought now affecting all parts of South Australia he cannot insist on the terms of the apprenticeship agreement being carried out by farmers situated as you are ... It therefore remains with you and the lad to make such arrangements as you may mutually agree upon.[58]

Both of these letters were dated 23 October 1914, reflecting how the drought impacted upon specific districts to varying degrees, within a broader region.

Although Field expressed regret that apprentices 'should have to face the season that is likely to prove the worst in the records of the State', the boys undoubtedly faced tough choices about their futures.[59] The war and very limited personal funds meant that there was practically no opportunity to return freely to Britain (although there were rare exceptions and a type of 'assisted passage' afforded by the war, which will be discussed below).[60] It was impressed upon the boys by Field that 'owing to the War and Drought large numbers of men and lads are out of work and there is at present scarcely any demand for labour'.[61] Field told Hanna that his apprentice 'would be well advised to remain with you (at whatever rate you can afford to pay)'. He wrote to another apprentice employed at nearby Crystal Brook: 'you may think it is breaking faith with you to ask you to accept a lower wage but it was impossible for the present serious situation to be anticipated when you were brought from England'.[62] The matter was further complicated by the varied legislation under which each apprenticeship agreement was processed – a young migrant's indenture could range from one to three years and once a contract expired there was no duty of care on the part of either the farmer or the government. The scheme's earliest participants who held one-year contracts could have found themselves unemployed as early as June 1914, regardless of the drought.

The way in which boys responded to the suspension of their contracts varied, as was demonstrated in the burgeoning new tract of agricultural land where Williams asserts drought 'told with melancholy effect': the Murray Mallee.[63] The farm apprenticeship recruitment brochure had advised that:

> Each boy will be expected to be useful about the house, and should remember that willingness in this direction will insure a kindly regard from the employer and his wife, which may lead them to give a helping hand to enable him to make his first start at farming on his own account'.[64]

However, despite this expectation of the apprentices and the government's reference checking of the masters, it seems that few boys were embraced in their host's household. One exception was Alexander Simpson, who was placed with John Fielding at Lameroo. Upon his arrival, Simpson wrote to Field that 'from first acquaintance I think I will get on first-class', and so it came to pass. This is evident from the tender letter the farmer sent to Field four years later, after Private Simpson had died of disease at 0030 hours on 12 November 1918, just 30 minutes after the conclusion of Armistice Day: '[Alex] looked upon my wife and me as his father and mother … In any event we should like to have [his medals] and value them in memory of the boy'.[65] Back in November 1914, Simpson had accepted a particularly low rate of five shillings per week, earning the Immigration Officer's praise: 'You are … taking a very sensible view of the position, and are to be commended … The good times will come again, and your consideration for Mr Fielding in the present serious position of his affairs will no doubt then be rewarded'.[66] Sadly, Simpson did not survive the war and was therefore unable to reap this reward.

Simpson's attitude was in stark contrast to the way in which his peers from the Kibble Farm School, friends George Bickerstaff and Joseph McQueen, handled their situations, with Edwin Wray at Lameroo and Alfred Gum at Pinnaroo respectively. Although Bickerstaff begrudgingly accepted a reduction in pay to 10 shillings per week, his master reported that he was unable to 'rouse him up to a sense of duty'.[67] Wray wrote to Field that one day, 'out of an hour and a quarter that I watched [Bickerstaff] did five minutes['s work], he sat down for over a half-hour, then got on his pony and rode about the paddock till time to come home'.[68] The apprentice was given notice and was fortunate to pick up some other work around Lameroo, including with the son of a member of parliament, who perhaps felt a sense of duty to keep the boy employed.[69]

Rather than accept a pay cut, Bickerstaff's mate McQueen said he would be 'willing to take another situation for a time and then return to [Gum] when prospects look brighter'.[70] Heedless of high unemployment, McQueen broke his contract, declaring that 'it is a different agreement to what he signed in Scotland' and that he would give himself a 'holiday' because 'I have not seen Pinnaroo since coming to it'.[71] Both of these boys were effectively left to fend for themselves, as was the Immigration Officer's inclination once the drought set in.

The way in which the Immigration Officer handled the situation for Murray Mallee apprentice William Suss was even more remarkable. Suss was first sent to Michael McCormack at Parilla and then Walter Hawker at Anama Station in the mid-north, but both engagements fell through. Suss returned to Adelaide, where the government took him in at the Domestic Helpers' Home at Norwood. The drought, war and Suss's sheer 'incapacity and lack of energy and intelligence' meant that 'it is considered that in the end he would cost the State more than his return passage money if allowed to remain here'.[72] Despite the war blocking most immigration, he was sent home on the RMS *Otway* at his own expense.[73] Suss was, however, a rare exception, and a return journey to Britain was not even entertained when others enquired.[74]

Repercussions

'Of course you have to take the Rough with the Smooth', was Frederick Ward's summation of the conditions he faced as one of South Australia's British farm apprentices on the eve of the First World War.[75] Ward's matter-of-fact remark understates the sudden reversal in the agricultural industry from a 'scarcity of labor [*sic*]' in the 1913 season to there being 'scarcely any demand for labour' in the 1914 season.[76]

This needs to be taken into consideration when accounting for the fact that more than three quarters of the British farm apprentices enlisted to fight with the Australian Imperial Force (AIF) during the First World War. The proportion of British-born soldiers in the AIF was relatively high in general but, as demonstrated above, the Great Eastern Drought provided a strong motivation for the apprentices to enlist during 1914–1915.[77] Here was an opportunity to return to Europe that had been denied to all but the likes of Suss.[78] The Great Eastern Drought should, in fact, be taken into account when evaluating the motivations for enlistment of any farm labourers from affected areas, not just these young migrants.[79] Eighteen farm apprentices made the ultimate sacrifice during the war and some are commemorated on memorials in country South Australia, as well as on the National War Memorial in Adelaide and Australian War Memorial in Canberra.[80] Of those who remained in South Australia during the war, it appears that few completed their apprenticeship; they instead drifted to employment elsewhere, including Robert Bradley, who was killed while working for the railways in May 1915.[81]

Nonetheless the Great Eastern Drought was short-lived and, as Williams surmises, 'one bad season was not enough to absorb the vapour of optimism'.[82] In May 1918 Private Christopher Hannant, who had been apprenticed at Port Broughton, wrote to Immigration Officer Field from London that he 'could see a vision: a nice home on a bonza farm by a river with a Tray Bon Wife and few Little Hannants running around'.[83] Field replied in September:

> I do not know that the picture that presented itself to you of a 'bonza' farm etc. is so much in the clouds after all ... when you return I am sure the Government will do all that is possible to assist you to make the dream a reality ... We have been having excellent seasons in South Australia since you left and the promise for this year is exceptionally good.[84]

A few former farm apprentices took advantage of the state's soldier settlement scheme to go back on the land after repatriation, such as Private Herbert Jarrett MM, who returned to Cleve.[85] As Williams has written, 'rural territorial expansion' was still an unquestioned aim in the mid-1920s and when the demand for agricultural labour intensified once again, Liberal Premier Henry Barwell revived the British farm apprenticeship scheme.[86] Approximately 1450 'Barwell Boys' arrived from 1922 to 1924, followed by about 125 'Little Brothers' in 1927–1929. They too would encounter the 'Rough with the Smooth' during their apprenticeships, including the onset of the Great Depression, but not the challenge presented by the unique combination of an extraordinary drought and unforeseen world war.

6

Eyre Peninsula on the eve of the Great War
A rural dimension

JILL ROE

The distinctive Eyre Peninsula triangle was home to Indigenous groups for many thousands of years before the landing of the first Europeans in 1839. The suggestion about contributing something to this collection led me first to the pages of the *Adelaide Chronicle*, as this weekly newspaper was where those on the Eyre Peninsula turned when we wanted to know about the wider world in the 1950s. The *Chronicle* was founded as far back as 1858 and lasted until 1975, by which time I had long since left the west coast, as we used to call it.

The *Chronicle* was the most impressive of the newspapers that came our way. The others were local papers but, as it turned out, they contained more information of relevance, probably because the *Chronicle* was published in Adelaide and was state-wide in coverage. Moreover, although there were several local papers published on Eyre Peninsula in 1914, there was not that much of wider interest in them for the *Chronicle* to draw upon. There may have been a local government structure in place by then, but it was mainly there for cost-saving purposes. The 12 counties in the state's Western Division at the 1911 census were thinly populated, with an overall population at that time of 13,389, of which the largest was the fast-growing municipal area Lincoln (presumably Port Lincoln) with a population of 3203 persons, and the smallest the interior division Le Hunte with only three persons recorded, a situation which would soon change when the Port Lincoln-Ceduna railway went through in 1913.[1]

Three main newspapers have been selected to find 'a rural dimension' to South Australia on the eve of the Great War. What they had to say depended to a large extent on where they were located and when they were founded. The oldest, *The West Coast Recorder*, was a weekly published in Port Lincoln from 1904 until 1942 (its circulation was 1250), with the ambitious subtitle '*The West Coast Recorder and Eyre Peninsula Chronicle*' from 1912. (The *Port Lincoln Times* came later, from 1927.) The *Eyre's Peninsula Tribune*, published at Cowell halfway up the east coast out of dissatisfaction with the *Recorder's* coverage of that area, dates from 1910 and, like the *Port Lincoln Times*, is still in publication, albeit at Cleve. Soon after, from about halfway up the west coast, came the *Streaky Bay Sentinel*, at first appended to the *West Coast Recorder* and from 1912 a stand-alone publication. Distance alone ensured that they did not speak with one voice. At first impression, *The West Coast Recorder* was the worldliest of the three, the *Eyre's Peninsula Tribune* the most self-contained, and the *Streaky Bay Sentinel* too recent to have established a distinctive voice.

It might be thought that such publications will have little to tell us about the reactions of country people to the coming of the Great War. It is true that they mostly did not do so until quite late. For example, the *Eyre's Peninsula Tribune* was very much a local paper and, it seems, scarcely mentioned European affairs until July 1914. But from early August there was usually a detailed column headed 'The War'. Farmers might not wish to

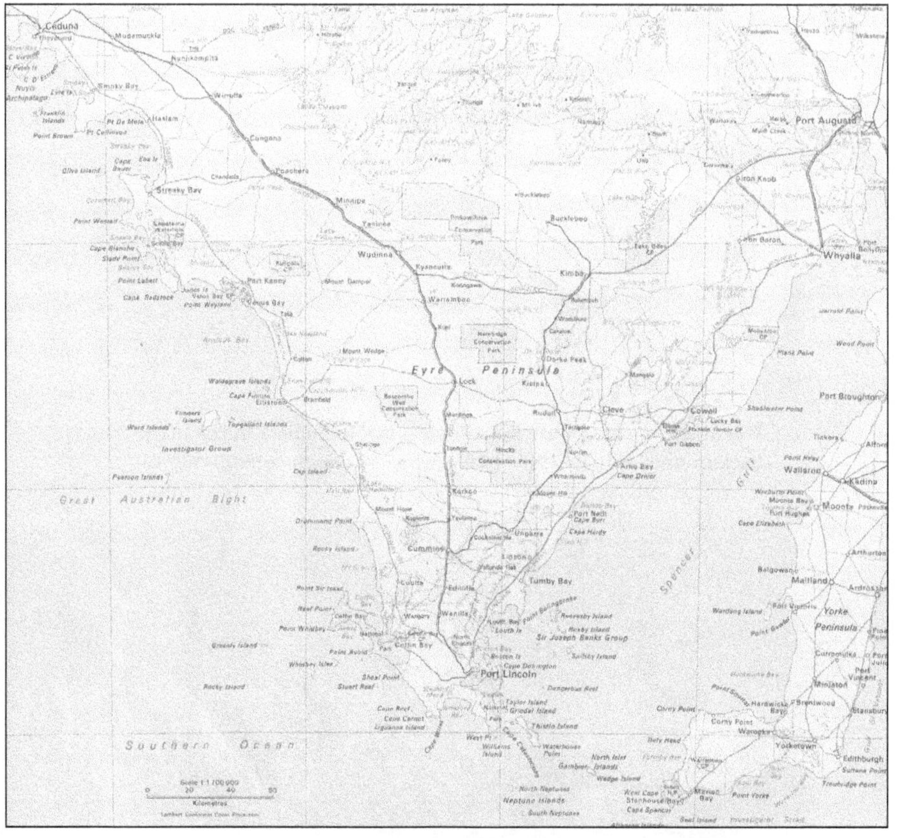

Map of Eyre Peninsula from the 1896 *Atlas of South Australia*.
[Mapland, Department of Environment, Water and Natural Resources]

read it but there it was – and they (or their wives) probably did. After all, before radio and television, the newspaper was the main source of the information increasingly sought and, as the war historian C.E.W. Bean put it in his classic work *On The Wool Track* (1910), the further out they were, the more eagerly they devoured whatever newsprint came their way.[2]

Wheat carting at Cowell, Eyre Peninsula; Methodist Church in the background, c. 1900–1915. [SLSA, Arthur M. Trengrove PRG 1480/7/64]

Horse drawn 4/6 foot stripper, with kangaroo dog atop. Near Port Lincoln, c. 1914. [SLSA, Port Lincoln Collection B 54073]

Nor can it be assumed that country people were indifferent or hostile to news of far-off wars. That came later. In early 1914 they could have had little idea of what a European war might bring, socially or economically. And they were empire loyalists. Empire loyalism was strong in South Australia, and especially so in recently settled places like Eyre Peninsula. If Britain was at war, so were they.

According to the first editorial in the *Adelaide Chronicle* for 1914, however, optimism prevailed: 'As a community we are entering on the New Year under the happiest auspices'. With the prospect of a good harvest and high prices, there was every reason to maintain 'a smiling countenance and a cheerful mind'. Caution was justified, but the demand for wheat was unlikely to go down and the recourse to strikes would surely diminish, given the spirit of justice and humanitarianism, 'which is after all the spirit of the age'.[3] Seven months later, by 8 August 1914, the *Chronicle*'s coverage of European affairs had become extensive.[4] There were graphics of the Austro-Hungarian leaders and detailed estimates of the relative fighting strengths of Austria, Hungary and Serbia, also recognition of the Russian and German forces waiting in the wings. The situation was alarming; but how things might develop was as yet impossible to say.

Anti-war sentiments were as yet few and far between in the media on the eve of the war. One bold reader did ask how it was that in such a mild and prosperous society there could be talk of war. This was in response to a survey of Australian defence forces by General Ian Hamilton in March 1914, sponsored by the Committee of Imperial Defence. In 1910 Lord Kitchener had found problems with Australia's military structure, advising its restructure; General Hamilton's task was to examine 'whether or not Australia [was] getting good value for the money annually expended'.[5] He had a straightforward answer to the reader: there would always be a threat of war, and although Australia might seem far from danger, it occupied a new part of the world, and there could be no certainty of peace with Asia.[6]

If there is little evidence of anti-war sentiment, there was not much sign of pro-war sentiment either, even of anti-German sentiment, at least at first. Distance itself was protective and the British navy was there to reassure even those living on the most remote coastlines. In fact, there was talk in early 1914, about making Boston Bay – Port Lincoln's harbour – a sub-naval base, for which it would have been quite suitable; but nothing came of it, and it is unlikely to have arisen from pro-war sentiment.[7] Moreover, a Royal Commission into the colony's wharves and jetties in 1911 had found that some of them were in excellent condition, so there was little cause for anxiety.[8] It is a cliché of regional history to say that country people pay little attention to politics. This is not quite right. They pay attention to the politics that affect them, and that means politics of a different kind.[9] It is easy to miss the difference. An advantage of a sharply defined topic is that we can see it more clearly, and especially is this so if the topic has within it one of history's most dramatic contrasts, the contrast between the world as it was before and at the onset of the Great War. It is no wonder its dimensions took people by surprise. Even so, it did not take long for the locals to organise patriotic rallies, as at Streaky Bay in August 1914.[10]

Local newspapers as a source of information and opinion have their limitations, and local newspapers must pay attention to local affairs. In the country that has mostly meant sport, the weather and the crops, and that distinctive rhythm of rural life. Even in my day, few readers of the local papers were driven by interest in state or national affairs; indeed, it was thought rather sissy to be concerned, unless some major issue impinged, for example the British nuclear tests being conducted in the interior at that time. The *Chronicle* was aware of more than such things as disquieting news from Turkey and Bulgaria – it was also aware of 'a marked falling off' of immigration, for instance, which affected the size of the labour market.[11] And letters to the editors were not what they are today, a matter for regret from the historian's point of view. If the letters to the editor of the *Chronicle* and the Cowell *Tribune* are a good guide to public opinion, which may be doubted since there were far fewer than today, what concerned readers mostly towards mid-1914 was the need for a new jetty south of Cowell and a railway connecting it to the interior.[12]

Until mid-1914, the optimistic local outlook prevailed. In January, departing Governor Sir Day Bosanquet, in office for five years and a promoter of the state's rights, visited the Peninsula and proclaimed Port Lincoln's 'romantic part' in the state's history was over. Instead, he spoke of an awakening awareness of the state's Western Division, the immense areas of arable land yet to be opened up, the necessity for closer settlement and the importance of immigration, all of which reinforced the commercial attractions of 'one of the finest harbours in the world'.[13] His positive views were largely sustained by Sir Henry Galway, the incoming governor, when he responded to his official welcome in April 1914.[14] In London, Australia's national representative, Sir George Reid, voiced similar comments.[15] But then in early July came 'shock and outrage' at the news of a murderous attack on the Archduke Franz Ferdinand and his wife in Sarajevo. Even so, it was still a matter in the *Chronicle* of 'the ill-fated Hapsburgs'.[16]

The curtain was rising

How would these distant events look to country people? Perspectives varied and it is hard to say. But one point may be assumed. The further away from Adelaide, the slower an informed response would be. The railway was still being built in the interior. Sometimes the weather prevented boats from landing along the coast, as at Elliston, a port some 170 kilometres west of Port Lincoln towards Ceduna. And often those few who had recently settled in such distant parts were unable to move due to lack of money.

Nonetheless that appeared to be a narrowly based stereotype. The *Streaky Bay Sentinel* may have been the furthest west and the youngest of the four papers under review, but in due course it would offer a substantial coverage of war news. The issue of August 14 carried a column summarising the content of war telegrams received daily from Adelaide. From this résumé of the situation in Europe, readers would learn that the first battle between the French and the Germans resulted in a French victory but 'the carnage was awful'. Anti-German sentiment was by then reportedly strong, but so was faith in the British navy. And it was here, in a war telegram, that local readers would learn that Lord Kitchener had expressed his 'grateful thanks' to Australia for its offer to help and expressed his confidence in the ability of Australian soldiers.[17] The war telegrams column in the *Streaky Bay Sentinel* was a form of catch-up, but a telling one.

There are further considerations. Enthusiasm for armed service was high at first, but not for long. South Australia had been the home of opposition to registration with military services pre-war, and whether or not enthusiasm for joining up when war was actually declared was ever high is a moot point.[18] Most likely, however, if it seemed so, it was among the 'townies', and decreasingly applicable to country boys, who were needed for the wheat harvest. These are big questions in Australian history and best approached through issues such as conscription, which did not arise until later.

On the eve of the war the population of Eyre Peninsula was as well informed as could reasonably be expected. I wish I could draw on family experience at this point but both my grandfathers died young, as did some of their sons. Although this was the era of large families, many of these families did not become involved in the military. It was not until World War II that the youngest members joined the armed services.

Cowell: when the boat comes in

The war and other news mostly reached Eyre Peninsula by boat. In the towns, sizable pubs marked – and still mark – the landing points, as at Cowell where a handsome hotel still graces the town (and its website).[19] At Tumby Bay there were two jetties and two pubs: the Tumby Bay Hotel and the Commercial Hotel. At Port Lincoln two large hotels were built close by the jetties (though the first of these no longer serves its original purpose, a spanking new one probably does). Likewise, on the west coast, jetties still serve social purposes, as have the jetties at Dutton Bay and at Streaky Bay.

What none of the pubs now do is serve as de facto post offices. The Commonwealth took over the postal services in 1901 and hence the distribution of mail. Probably it happened a bit later on Eyre Peninsula, where the mail remained a matter of 'when the boat comes in'. That meant from Adelaide – which was linked to Darwin from the 1860s – or, so far as Cowell was concerned, Wallaroo. The ships up the west coast had a particularly hard time of it, as did those contractors who moved

The old jetty and town of Tumby Bay, Eyre Peninsula, 1909. [SLSA, Searcy Collection PRG 280/1/6/351]

the mail into the interior. The contractors conveying the mails from Port Augusta to the west and north-west through the Gawler Ranges suffered 'extreme hardship'.[20] Further into the interior, where population was even more thinly spread and the rail was yet to make its way, such mail as there was – there could not have been much for the County of Le Hunte (Wudinna), with its recorded population of three in 1911 – would have been delivered by horse-drawn coach, travelling from hotel to hotel or pausing for rest at small general stores in the middle of nowhere. Altogether it seems surprising that the mail got through.

Such were the ways that country people 'kept up'. Letters from friends and family on 'the other side', the linking shipping services and the horse-drawn coaches on land ensured that they were quite well-informed pre-1914. For colonists as recent as the small settlers on Eyre Peninsula before 1914, some family and friends might still be somewhere in the Northern Hemisphere. The Laube family, for example, left southern Silesia for South Australia in 1854; Fred and Lottie Laube came to Eyre Peninsula from Port Pirie in the early twentieth century, having been allotted a block of land in the new hundred of Koppio. There seems to have been little awareness of these German settlers as different.[21]

The importance of difference was more evident if we think of the position of Aboriginal people at that time. It is not easy to do so, however, as by 1914 only one of the missions remained, the Lutheran mission at Koonibba beyond Ceduna. Aboriginal people nowadays are divided as to whether the Lutheran mission was beneficial in those early days and the sources are limited.[22] Maybe it is a matter of place. The colonisers were inclined to take a positive view, as in a rare comment constructed for a conference booklet in 1914, based on Aboriginal experience outside Whyalla, which is only to be expected, but also quite possibly justified to some extent. A Royal Commission investigating missions and the 'whole question of the South Australian aborigines' visited Koonibba in 1914 and was favourably impressed.[23] Likewise a Lutheran delegation inspected the mission in August 1914, and reported it to be in good hands and the natives 'very loyal'. What Aboriginal people thought is unclear, though many partook of the Lord's Sacrament and some were able to converse on current politics and the war. One resident, who was crippled, was said to be 'a faithful member of the Lutheran church' who always carried his Bible with him.[24]

Like so many aspects of the Eyre Peninsula experience of 1914, more research is needed. To date only two substantial studies in the social history of the entire region have been undertaken, of the Koonibba mission to the west of Ceduna by Peggy Brock, and of schooling in the Franklin Harbour district to 1900 by Kay Whitehead and Ben Wadham.[25] From the latter study we learn that there were nine one-teacher schools in the district at that time, with mostly women teachers, generally young locals, unqualified but still very competent and much valued for their social skills. Children benefited accordingly. The main point here, however, is simply the extent of closer settlement pre-1914 thus evidenced.

Streaky Bay: from mission to church

No account of Eyre Peninsula at this time would be satisfactory without reference to the churches, most of which would have been protestant. One reason for looking at Streaky Bay is that there has long been a significant Catholic presence, although one source suggests that there were only five Catholic families in the Streaky Bay area in 1914.[26] Maybe that would have made a difference to local attitudes to the coming European war? With fewer than three years of press evidence to draw on – as previously noted, the *Sentinel* became a stand-alone publication in 1912 – it is especially hard to say. More likely the Catholic residents, of whom there were few, were as loyalist as the rest of the population.

Until 1914, Streaky Bay Catholicism was part of a home mission field extending from Port Augusta and Port Lincoln to as far west as Fowler's Bay. Priests with responsibility for such a vast area were unable to make regular visits. But in some ways that meant they made greater efforts to attend to their flock, and were the more appreciated. It was an event when they arrived, and it was often the case that numbers of both children and adults were baptised. When Father Kelly was farewelled from the area in 1914 (to be replaced by Father O'Halloran from the Port Augusta diocese), he estimated that during his ten years in the field he had travelled 60,000 miles by buggy and automobile and written 10,000 letters in the course of his work.[27] When Father Jorgensen, who was about to return to Port Lincoln, heard that there were Catholic workers beyond Eucla who could not get in for a service, he re-packed his bags and turned back to attend to them. Father Kelly and Father Jorgensen left Northern Eyre Peninsula in 1914, satisfied that they were leaving the Catholic mission in good shape.[28]

1914 seems to mark a turning point for of the churches at Streaky Bay. The first resident Catholic priest was appointed in that year, with a defined diocese, from Talia, near Venus Bay and Warramboo in the south-west, to Fowlers Bay and beyond. The first notices of Sunday services appeared in the *Sentinel* at Streaky Bay and Calca in June, and an impressive church, St Canute's, was completed in 1912. St Augustine's, an equally sizeable Anglican church, opened that same year. No passer-by could fail to notice these buildings in a town like Streaky Bay, being smaller and farther out and having few substantial buildings.

As well, there were now more resident clergy to add cachet to the town and to serve the needs of the north-west. The clergy became more prominent in the press, with many social duties recorded there. When a patriotic demonstration was held mid-August 1914, Canon Howard, Father O'Halloran, the Reverends Rowe and Sanders, and Mr Oborn all delivered 'stirring patriotic addresses' after a rally in the main street.[29] They deplored the fact that Britain had been drawn into the war but asserted that she had been forced into it. Something of the tone and quality of the *Sentinel* as a local paper will be apparent here, and a pointer to why, in the departing words of Father Kelly in 1914, 'there is no such thing as sectarianism here'.[30]

Port Lincoln: a 'might-have-been' capital

In the beginning some thought Port Lincoln should be South Australia's capital. It fronted a large region itself and Boston Bay was a splendid harbour. But the idea did not last long – there was not enough water for domestic purposes, or to support a substantial population. It was not until the 1960s that Port Lincoln was declared a city. In 1914 the urban area may have been the largest on the Peninsula but the population had not yet reached 4000, nor did it have a conspicuous cultural identity. However, until the development of Whyalla in the 1940s, it was always the main urban area; and it did make a distinct impression. Looking back, I would say it was of pride.

Pride is not an easy thing to pin down, especially in times past. The local Port Lincoln paper had a turbulent history, due to changes of ownership, but a kind of cultural stability came with the *West Coast Recorder and Eyre's Peninsula Chronicle* (dating from 1912 to 1942), and the region's settled character meant plenty of local pride in its pages. It also makes it seem rather dull, to an outsider at least. There is a limit to the appeal of sport and meetings about issues like the water supply, important as the latter was by then.

One oddity of the South Australian story that stands out is 'the institute'. Predating colonisation, this was an expression of the British self-help movement. By the 1860s the South Australian government was supporting a hybrid system of book-borrowing institutes open to the general public and public libraries with reference books available on-site to subscribers only. This lasted for a century or more. The Port Lincoln Institute – accessed by a walkway hidden between the Town Hall and the shops in Port Lincoln – was one of the stronger institutes in the state. Otherwise readers may have had access to the book boxes sent out by the South Australian Institute to more remote areas.[31] The Institute was an indication both of Port Lincoln's comparative age and status by 1914, and of the youth and thinness of white colonisation elsewhere at that time, perhaps also of the significance of newspapers.

The coverage of cultural events around Port Lincoln was of increasing significance over time. So too was participation in cultural life. There, as elsewhere in rural and regional Australia, a pianist, a fiddler or a singer were much appreciated, and bands often travelled significant distances to perform at dances and concerts up the country. The ladies' columns of the *West Coast Recorder* reported these events in impressive detail.[32] The Australian Ball, held in Port Lincoln Institute on 31 July 1914, in aid of the Church of St Mary and the Angels, was deemed a marvel of floral decoration and a brilliant success, with crowds reportedly turned away for lack of space.[33] Many such events could be mentioned, at places large and small, but the lure of those at Port Lincoln was perhaps greatest.[34]

Eyre Peninsula on the eve of the Great War, though an area of relatively recent settlement, was doing quite well. Cowell was an established rural and fishing centre. Despite the extent of its surrounding farmlands, Streaky Bay was slowly making its way. Port Lincoln was still the premier port, priding itself on its cultural vitality and its role as an entrepot. And the railway line being built to Ceduna would open up the hitherto undeveloped interior. Moreover, thanks to well-produced newspapers, the residents of the Peninsula were everywhere alerted to the wider

A group from the Australasian Ornithologists' Union constructing their camp during a trip to Warunda, Eyre Peninsula, October 1909. The ornithologists enjoyed press coverage of their activities. [SLSA, Warunda Collection B 58284]

world and its challenges. There can be little doubt that they were aware the outbreak of the war would bring challenges, but the voluntarism of South Australia and the importance of food production would to some extent protect these remote rural communities from the war's worst horrors. As well, its relatively recent settlement meant that most of its men folk were probably a little too old for war service or still too young. No doubt these factors go some way towards explaining my own limited awareness of war on Eyre Peninsula in the first half of the twentieth century, and the sense that what Bean liked to think of as 'the real Australians' survived there.

7

Town planning in the 'Garden City of the South'

The state of play to 1914

CHRISTINE GARNAUT

The turn of the twentieth century ushered in the modern town planning movement that established itself in Australia in the following decades. The 1910s in particular was a period of 'extraordinary activity in establishing town planning as a vital social concern and issue for public policy'.[1] Before the emergence of the idea of town planning, the private sector largely drove development. Landowners operated within a laissez-faire or 'go as you please' framework, and the decisions and interventions that they made with regard to the layout of cities, towns and subdivisions, the provision of public infrastructure and services, and the siting and design of buildings and structures, were subject to limited legislative control.[2] Consequently, development occurred in an ad hoc and piecemeal fashion. Private developers rarely looked to the future needs of a community and often acted without regard to the effect of their developments on the immediate or wider built or natural environment, or on the health and wellbeing of the population.

This chapter surveys the physical planning and development of Adelaide from the foundation of South Australia in 1836 through to c. 1914. The discussion begins with a brief introduction to the Adelaide Plan (1837) and to how it was modified once on the ground. An overview follows, derived from a range of sources including plans, maps, letters and photographs, of how the city of Adelaide and its suburbs developed in the decades preceding the First World War. Key urban challenges and problems that arose in the nineteenth and early twentieth century are identified. The concept of town planning, which emerged in Britain and Continental Europe in the late nineteenth century and was promoted internationally as an approach to ameliorating living and working conditions in urban environments, is introduced.

A textbook colonial plan

South Australia was founded at a time when the role of the old orders of government and religion were under question, liberalism and laissez-faire capitalism were on the rise, individual rights and freedoms were being advocated, ideas about what had gone astray in the settlement of other colonies were being advanced, and alternative models of colonisation were in the air.[3] Among the many promoters of fresh conceptual frameworks for colonisation was Englishman Edward Gibbon Wakefield (1796–1862), whose theory of 'systematic colonisation' the British Government took up in its instructions for the foundation of the province of South Australia.[4] Under the Wakefield-inspired scheme, the province would be independent of Britain, self-supporting and a place of religious and political freedom. Land would be sold, at a set price, and the profits used to send labourers on free passage to the colony. The price of land would be high in order to avoid large tracts being purchased for pastoral pursuits and to encourage more intensive usage.[5] Labourers would have the opportunity, in time, to save enough from their earnings to purchase land of their own. The aim was to achieve 'a balance between land, labour and capital' and to promote free enterprise, respectability and self-improvement.[6]

The settlement of South Australia extended the 'southern rim' of the British Empire.[7] Britain had been furthering its colonial assets since the seventeenth century, viewing the imperialist outposts that it established as civilizing influences and bastions of trade and defence. Intentionally, it established a major town and supporting administrative structures in each of its new colonies. The town's physical layout was informed chiefly by Lord Shaftesbury's 'Grand Modell' of colonial planning, which routinely incorporated:

> wide streets laid out in geometric, usually grid-iron form, usually on an area of one square mile; public squares; standard sized rectangular plots ...; some plots reserved for public purposes; and a physical distinction between town and country, usually by common land or an encircling green belt.[8]

The Plan of Adelaide (1837) reflected these key design elements as well as other influences.[9] It has been described as the most sophisticated international expression of the 'Grand Modell' and as Australia's 'best known textbook [colonial] plan'.[10]

Like Wakefield's theory, the Plan of Adelaide was 'systematic'.[11] It had three distinct parts: a core of town lands, intended for living, administrative and commercial purposes (referred to as the city, it included South and North Adelaide); an encircling belt of public parklands that also extended into the river valley dividing the core; and a periphery of suburban lands. By the end of the first decade of settlement, the parklands served the additional purposes of acting as a natural buffer between the core and the periphery, of separating the planned centre from the unplanned outer areas, and of providing respite from the

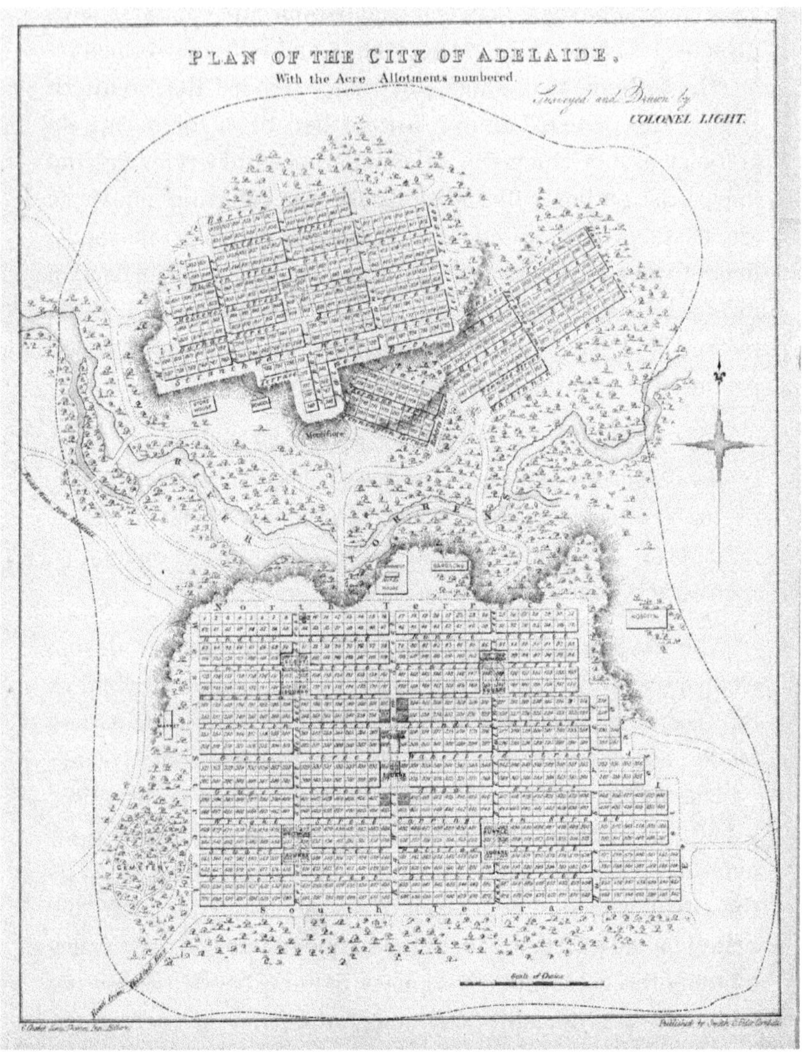

Plan of the City of Adelaide with acre allotments numbered and streets and squares named, published by Smith & Elder, Cornhill, London, in 1839. [NLA 231437040]

built form. The Plan's three parts contributed collectively to its distinctive morphology that ultimately distinguished Adelaide from the other Australian capital cities.[12]

Adelaide's layout was based on a grid and comprised streets, public squares and building allotments set down on near-flat terrain.[13] The plan provided 1042 town lots, each of one acre. Seven hundred were in South Adelaide and the remainder in North Adelaide. A river, to be known as the Torrens, and the expansive reserved area on its reaches, separated the two parts.

South Adelaide was symmetrical, apart from the south-east side where the boundary stepped with the land contours. Eleven streets ran east-west and six north-south. None was narrower than 66 feet, the length of the surveyor's chain. The bounding terraces, all 100 feet wide, overlooked parkland. There were five squares. A site for a cathedral was marked to the south of the central square, named in time for the reigning British monarch, Queen Victoria, and two town acres were reserved for government offices on its northern side. A further two acres were set aside, for unspecified purposes, on the south. A site for a municipal town hall was allocated on the corner of what became King William and Pirie Streets. A cemetery, market and Botanic Gardens were earmarked for the western belt of parkland. Government House, positioned in generous grounds of ten acres, terminated the northern vista along the north-south axis. Military barracks were located not far from the governor's residence. A hospital was proposed for a location in parklands to the north-east.

North Adelaide comprised three essentially rectangular parcels of land, offset to relate to the topography, to the river and to views to South Adelaide. The largest portion was graced by a centrally positioned square officially titled Wellington

Square. A school and a government store were proposed for the parklands south-west of the square. In North Adelaide, as in South Adelaide, edges of numerous land parcels fronted parkland. The plan suggested that all of the squares, as well as the parklands, would be amply vegetated, although no planting layouts or plant species were recommended.

The port for the town, Port Adelaide, was about six miles away and was approached by a diagonal track that connected into the north-west corner of the town grid. The road to the port became a well-used thoroughfare, one of several diagonal routes that emerged in the early years to take travellers away from or into the capital. The others were from the south-west corner to Holdfast Bay, renamed Glenelg in 1839, and towards the Torrens Valley in the north-east and the Adelaide Hills in the south-east.

Implementing the Plan

Wakefield advanced the notion of an orderly approach to land sales, alienation and settlement, and proposed that land would be surveyed before it was alienated. But when the first wave of colonists arrived in South Australia in December 1836, the site for the principal town had not been decided, and its plan was not finalised. Although these matters were resolved quickly, rural land, critical to establishing the colony's agricultural focus and workforce, was unavailable before 1840.

Once the site for Adelaide was surveyed in March 1837 the holders of preliminary land orders, purchased in London, selected their town acres. All unselected blocks were later sold by auction, either to colonists who had already moved to South Australia or to absentee landlords. Purchasers bought 'off the plan', before the extensively timbered plain was cleared sufficiently for the pattern of streets, allotments and squares to be easily distinguishable. That process took several years.

The majority of early development occurred in the northern section of South Adelaide, particularly in the north-west corner, close to where the road to the port cut into the street grid, and to the River Torrens, the sole source of fresh water. Surveyor-General Light set up camp near the Torrens, promoting 'a long straggling village of huts and tents ... until the town was clearly marked out. ... [U]ntil March, 1839, private dwellings were allowed in the parks'.[14] An Immigration Depot of thirty-five double cottages, known as Buffalo Row, was established in the parklands to the west of the town in late 1837, within water-carting distance of the river.[15]

In 1838 Adelaide's *Register* newspaper described Hindley Street as far as Morphett Street as 'decidedly the first street [for business] in the city ... [North Terrace] as one of the most desirable and valuable quarters of the town ... [and King William Street as] a rising situation'.[16] Additionally, the paper noted that intermittent development was emerging on blocks along West Terrace, Currie Street to Light Square, and Rundle Street to Stephens Place. The connection of the Holdfast Bay Road into the south-west corner of the town contributed to limited early settlement in that sector, where South Terrace was the favoured location for the earliest domestic buildings.[17]

Early modifications

The experience of actually living in Adelaide and of carrying out the activities of everyday life soon led to modifications to the physical plan, although its underlying physical structure was preserved. A survey map prepared in 1841, by George Strickland Kingston, engineer, surveyor, architect for early Adelaide buildings including Government House and the gaol, and Town

Surveyor for the Corporation of Adelaide, reveals the types of changes that were implemented.[18]

At the time of Kingston's survey approximately 6000 people lived in the city of Adelaide. His detailed map illustrates that a number of town acres had been subdivided into blocks of differing sizes and shapes, particularly in the north-west sector, where the majority of people lived. Additionally, about thirty mostly north-south roadways of varying widths had been cut through the town acres to make access streets and lanes, and to facilitate more convenient movement between the major thoroughfares. None of this development occurred in accordance with a formal plan, and legislation did not then exist to control subdivision or decisions about the location or width of streets – private developers acted simply according to their personal goals and desires.

The subdivision of town acres into smaller lots was driven by both circumstance and opportunism. As the site for the city was not selected or surveyed in advance of the arrival of would-be settlers from December 1836, the survey of the surrounding country land and consequently the occupation of rural areas were held up. Meanwhile people were living in tents and makeshift shelters waiting to purchase lots on which to build dwellings. The city survey was finished on 10 March 1837. Once land became available many of those who had purchased town acres saw the chance to capitalise on what was surely a pressure-cooker situation. They subdivided their acre(s) and named their price. So began an intense period of land speculation by individuals and land companies. One of the effects was to drive up prices.[19] Consequently, as rural land was opened up following the completion of the country survey in late 1839, those unable to afford a town allotment purchased blocks in the villages that had begun to emerge on the fringes of the parklands.

Kingston indicated the location and uses of the city's existing public and private buildings that served its burgeoning population. In addition to Government House, there were approximately 1900 private dwellings as well as shops, warehouses, churches and chapels, a bank, flour mills, workshops, a hospital, a gaol and military barracks. Kingston's depiction of private dwellings reveals one house per allotment, signaling a trend that became the norm as the city developed and expanded into residential areas beyond its parkland belt.

Kingston's survey confirmed the continuation of the early trend to build in the north-west corner. Then referred to as the 'West End', it was clearly the chief business and residential district, and was characterized by 'shops, hotels, places of entertainment and numerous eating houses'.[20] Hindley Street was the residential, retail, business and industrial hub. An 1841 visitor to Adelaide referred to the mixed-use character of the area, noting that in addition to houses there were about 200 stores, shops and warehouses.[21] However, a little over a decade later, with the growth of village settlements on Adelaide's eastern fringes, trade gradually began to shift to Rundle Street and its off-shoots.[22]

According to Kingston's map, elsewhere in the city in 1841 the original plan was largely intact although construction was intermittent, with virtually none in the south-east corner. Victoria Square stood 'in splendid isolation'.[23] Minimal development had occurred in North Adelaide, where the greatest concentration was to the south and close to the parklands. Capitalising on the largely residential character of the area, speculator John Barton Hack had laid out a subdivision on the southern side of Stanley Street.[24] One bridge, located towards the north-west corner of South Adelaide, connected the two parts of the city. An area on the northern side of the River Torrens was designated as the 'Aborigines location', one of several spaces 'allocated' to the local Kaurna community and visiting Aboriginal people.[25]

A city of contrasts

By June 1850, when newly arrived colonist Emily Clark observed that she had arrived in a 'city of contrasts', Adelaide's population had reached about 15,000 and South Australia was well on its way to being 'one of the most urbanised societies on earth'.[26] Clark remarked that:

> The city was much better and much worse than I expected. It was a surprise to find so many good shops and houses where we thought we should only find log huts and stores, but I was quite unprepared for the mud, and the wretched hovels close to well-built residences gave a most incongruous appearance to the streets.[27]

Another new arrival, Charles Barton, who reached Adelaide in December 1853, was equally surprised by aspects of the capital's development. In a letter written in 1854 to relatives in England, he explained how 'busy [and] over-civilised' a place Adelaide was, but expressed his distaste for its 'broad streets strewed with dust and floating straws'.[28] He enclosed a mud map illustrating key aspects of the city's layout and built environment as well as the location of his house at the east end of North Terrace. His drawing is a reminder of the original predominantly residential character of the south side of North Terrace. It also reinforces the ongoing concentration of settlement in South

Adelaide's northern sector, and clearly reveals the emerging hub of activity on the Hindley–Rundle Street axis and around their intersection with King William Street. Barton noted the location and proliferation of inns and taverns – there were 88 in 1850 – and drew attention to the villages established on Adelaide's perimeter.[29]

Photographer Townsend Duryea captured the extent of Adelaide's development in a panorama of images taken in 1865. They demonstrated that the city had taken on a permanent appearance with brick and stone buildings now replacing the temporary structures of the founding years. Apart from buildings, streetscapes and skylines, Dureya's photographs revealed the pattern of Adelaide's streets. They confirmed that the grid had been implemented and adhered to, and identified the spaces where land was still vacant. Additionally, they portrayed the generous spread of the city as South Adelaide faded along King William Street and North Adelaide emerged in the distance. They recorded, too, the distinctive belt of parklands that contained the city in shape and size, and provided its citizens with land for a range of pursuits.

Dureya's panorama depicted the shroud of development in villages beyond the city. About thirty were established by the mid-1860s.[30] They included Hindmarsh, Bowden, and Prospect, all established near the road to the port and to opportunities for employment, principally in cartage businesses. Thebarton provided work in its tanneries and brickworks. South of the parklands, Unley and Goodwood were within walking distance of jobs and services in Adelaide. To the east were Kensington, Marryatville and Norwood. Towards the north-east, a 'better class' of village was established at Walkerville where lots sold for £120 per acre compared with at Bowden where the selling price was £75. Beyond the suburban villages, each the nucleus of a later suburb, were the rural villages that included Mitcham, Klemzig and Tea Tree Gully.

Expansion and growth

Thomas Worsnop, Town Clerk of the Corporation of Adelaide between 1869 and 1897, included a detailed map of the city in his history of the municipality to 1877.[31] By then Adelaide was experiencing a period of expansion that revealed itself in a rise in public works, secondary industry, land subdivision (particularly south and east of the city) and a building boom.[32] The infrastructure, public spaces and buildings and other structures noted on his map were indicative of the expansion that was under way.

The 1877 map showed the extent to which mostly north-south as well as east-west streets and lanes had been cut into the original road pattern – the number had risen from 51 originally to over 360 – thus disrupting the grid of regularly sized one-acre allotments.[33] No part of the city had been spared, although the practice was less prevalent in the south-east sector and in North Adelaide.

Several roads and bridges, absent in the 1837 plan, now formally connected South and North Adelaide. In addition to the four main early routes into and away from Adelaide, numerous other roads were now marked in every direction through the parklands. They led to various destinations beyond their perimeter. A railway line to Glenelg ran south from Victoria Square along King William Street.

Aside from showing transportation routes, Worsnop's map identified a variety of public buildings and structures commensurate with Adelaide's expansion. These included

Government House and the military barracks, hospital and cemetery that were incorporated in the 1837 Plan, but also an orphanage and a lunatic asylum, exhibition building, university, museum, City Baths, Parliament House and railway station between North Terrace and the River Torrens. There was a waterworks building and valve house in the north-east parklands, a racecourse with grandstand in the east parklands, and a gaol, slaughterhouse, observatory, signal station and sheep markets to the west and north-west of the city. A space for 'The Oval' (Adelaide Oval) was designated north of the River Torrens.

When artist Edmund Gouldsmith painted a captivating scene of 'King William Street, Adelaide, 1885' from Victoria Square, Adelaide had all the vestiges of a capital city. Although streets were not yet sealed, infrastructure and services like reticulated water, deep drainage and gas lighting were in place. Public transport was available in the form of rail and horse-drawn tramways. Adelaide had a 'civic pride and corporate identity'.[34] The distinctive style and materials of its masonry and brick buildings helped to reinforce its role as the capital and to create a sense of place for its citizens. The towers on the Town Hall and General Post Office were local landmarks.[35] Adelaide was the administrative, commercial, industrial, financial and cultural hub of the colony. It was the place of everyday life for a substantial proportion of South Australia's population. People living in the villages and further afield went to the city to purchase goods, to attend to their personal and business affairs, and to utilise its facilities and visit its entertainment places.

However, the apparent serenity of Gouldsmith's scene belied the reality of the times.[36] In fact, by the mid-1880s, South Australia was experiencing the effects of a depression that eventually took hold nationally and internationally. Recovery was minimal until the first decade of the new century.

A new century: urban growth and the challenges of expansion

In 1901 approximately 40,000 people lived in the City of Adelaide.[37] The number remained static into the 1920s. By contrast, the suburban population rose steadily from around 141,000 in 1901 to about 199,000 by 1914.[38] In those years Adelaide's metropolitan area began a period of gradual and radial expansion from the centre into the previously subdivided areas, and in a north-westerly direction to Port Adelaide.[39] Expansion into new suburban areas prompted a mix of responses. Some argued that the moment was opportune to take stock of the physical condition of the city of Adelaide, where the majority of the population still lived, to study overseas trends in urban improvement and to apply lessons learnt from elsewhere, both in the areas being opened up for new development and in the city itself. Others protested against change on the grounds that Adelaide was renowned as an exemplar of colonial town planning and admired for its distinctive layout of gridded streets, punctuated by public squares and enveloped by parklands.

In 1901 the city of Adelaide's social composition was diverse, with all income groups represented within the city's boundaries.[40] Wealthy professionals and businessmen preferred to live in the eastern and southern sectors, especially along the terraces where they could enjoy views of the parklands. The West End housed the poorer families and their places of work – the brewery on Hindley Street, slaughterhouse in the parklands, and tanneries, glue, soap and candle manufacturers, whose premises were variously located. The laissez-faire approach to

Street scenes like this one of an unidentified street in the West End in the 1910s showed the effect of laissez-faire development in parts of nineteenth- and early twentieth-century Adelaide.
[History SA, SAGPC GN 01689]

development continued: the city council was responsible for infrastructure and facilities such as roads and public buildings and amenities like parks and gardens, but the rest was in the hands of the private sector.

The Council had very limited control over development, including the location and practices of industry, and the construction of houses or any other building type. Despite the health risks and constant complaints from residents about foul odours, noise and other industrial pollution, the Council did not have the power to remove activities such as boiling down works from the city. Slaughterhouses were moved out in 1908, with the introduction of the Metropolitan Abattoirs Act, but cows and dairies remained for some years after that. Despite the existence of Building Acts (1881, 1885 and 1911), there were few constraints on individuals. Consequently, jerry-building, speculation and overcrowding were rife.

In the suburbs, landowners arranged the subdivision of their land. Seeking the highest return for their investment, their usual practice was to engage a surveyor to divide the holding into streets and the maximum number of residential blocks. Under the Municipal Corporations Act of 1890 landowners were required to lodge plans of their proposal with their council; the council then submitted the proposals to the surveyor-general. Before the Control of Subdivision Act of 1917 there were virtually no grounds upon which a subdivision could be refused. Additionally, legislation was not in place to regulate block sizes or the provision of open space, shops, schools or other community facilities. Private investors did not normally set aside land for any of these purposes. Similarly, landowners were not concerned about design principles and did not take into consideration elements like tree-lined streets, vistas, or the siting of buildings to break views. The ad hoc layout of suburban subdivisions was in stark contrast with the structure and formality of the Adelaide Plan. Indeed, the opportunity to develop Adelaide's suburbs in an organised manner, reflective of the intent of the original plan, had not been grasped.

The expansion into the suburbs in the 1910s and up to the First World War (Table 1) put pressure on existing infrastructure and public transport and services such as reticulated water, deep drainage, gas and electricity. Electricity had been available from the late 1890s, and the rise in electric tramways from 1909 contributed to suburban growth as people took advantage of living in suburbs connected to the city by tram.[41] However, the provision of infrastructure, services and utilities was largely in private hands and, like the ad hoc manner of subdivision, was neither initiated nor controlled in an organised way.

Table 1. Location and number of houses erected in Adelaide and suburbs 1911–1914[42]

Location	1911	1912	1913	1914
Adelaide	12	20	41	56
Unley	394	483	442	359
Hindmarsh	62	70	75	52
Kensington/Norwood	54	61	62	44
St Peters	90	107	116	68
Thebarton	250	340	127	166
Burnside	100	237	121	277
Mitcham	90	106	149	212
Payneham	85	100	120	84
Prospect	160	230	228	121
West Torrens	112	176	149	183

Changes in the air

The situation regarding Adelaide's physical development mirrored what had been and was happening in other parts of Australia and, albeit not as severely, in North America and Europe, in the wake of the industrialisation and rapid urbanisation of cities. Responses overseas to the physical condition of industrialised cities and to the circumstances of their citizens, especially the working classes and the poor, took various forms.[43] In the search for ways to achieve order in the seemingly chaotic and haphazardly developed urban environments, new ideas emerged about the desirable qualities of cities and about their layout and functions. Overlooked elements like public open space were foregrounded, as were ideas about the aesthetics and beautification of cities, and their future regulation and administration. Such ideas were expressed and applied in different approaches and conceptual models, several of which were transmitted globally.[44] Their emphases varied. For example, the grand renewal of Paris that began under Baron von Haussmann from the 1850s created a city centre characterised by wide, tree-lined boulevards, low-rise buildings and a proliferation of open space.[45] However, to achieve the renewal of Paris, Haussmann removed the working classes from the heart of the city. Nonetheless the outcome was widely admired and the 'Haussmannisation' of cities was emulated elsewhere. The City Beautiful movement that emerged in North America around the turn of the nineteenth century focused on civic beautification and on the utility and functionality of cities.[46] On the other hand, the Garden City idea devised in England by Ebenezer Howard in the 1890s provided a more holistic and forward-looking model of urban development, which responded to human as well as to physical planning needs.[47]

At about the same time as Howard was promoting his idea, others in Continental Europe and in England were advocating the coordination, organisation and regulation of development in towns and cities or, in other words, what came to be known as town planning.[48] They understood town planning as a function of government and as a forward-looking, anticipatory process by which the current, and the future, needs of cities, towns and suburbs would be determined. Supporters of the concept argued that town planning was a coordinated process, requiring the cooperation of all organisations involved with providing infrastructure, transport and services, and a formal body with oversight and management of their activities. They maintained that legislation was essential to secure these outcomes.

Town Clerk of the City of Adelaide, Torrington George Ellery, ensured that the city council and South Australians generally heard about town planning. Ellery:

> made it his business to seek information and advice continually from municipalities in France, Germany, Canada, the United States and India as well as Britain. When councillors and Town Hall staff went on trips overseas, he encouraged them to investigate matters ... and to report in detail on what they found.[49]

After 1911, his *Annual Report* included a town planning section, in which he made reference to overseas and local town planning initiatives (especially legislative), to principal international figures involved and to contemporary publications.

However, the citizens of Adelaide were generally ambivalent about the need to apply ideas about town planning in their city. Most agreed that the capital had a *rus in urbe* character evident in the open city squares, parklands, formal public gardens and avenues of trees.[50] Interstate and overseas visitors praised the city. American author Mark Twain was positively glowing in his assessment. He recalled that travelling by carriage through the hills on the road from Melbourne:

> finally the mountain gateway opened and the immense plan lay spread out below and stretching away into dim distances ... On its near edge reposed the city. With wide streets, compactly built; with fine homes everywhere, embowered in foliage and flowers, and with imposing masses of public buildings nobly grouped and architecturally beautiful.[51]

Like Edmund Gouldsmith's 1885 painting, this scene looking north across Victoria Square to King William Street captures the character and perceived serenity of mid- to late-1880s Adelaide.

[Andrew Garran, *Picturesque Atlas of Australasia* (Sydney: Picturesque Atlas Publishing Company, 1888)]

Views like Twain's confirmed a popular sentiment and were supported by the self-interested landowners who argued that Adelaide already knew about and practised town planning.[52] The capital was renowned overseas for its layout. It was even referred to as the 'Garden City of the South'. But the protesters apparently did not look past the terraces beyond the parklands towards the haphazard and mostly ill-planned subdivisions, that lacked the order and open spaces of the Adelaide plan. Seemingly, they were blind also to the inner-city development that had created overcrowding and cramped, substandard living conditions, especially in the north-west and parts of the south-west sectors.

By contrast, advocates for town planning like Ellery acknowledged that while the original plan for the city was significant, its features had been ignored in late nineteenth and early twentieth century subdivisions. They recognised that town planning went beyond simply laying out a city, town or suburb, to encompass the appearance, utility and convenience of these places, as well as the comfort of their citizens.[53]

The government responded favourably to urgings from town planning promoters. In February 1913 Frank W. Young, Commissioner of Crown Lands, distributed a circular to all municipal bodies in Adelaide stating that the government was keen to improve the planning of suburbs.[54] A conference in July 1913, attended by Ryan, Young and delegates from each council, discussed what could be done.[55] Subsequently, the government established a committee to which it eventually passed the responsibility of drafting town-planning legislation for South Australia.

Meanwhile Ellery had another card up his sleeve. His 1912 *Annual Report* introduced Adelaide City councillors to Charles Reade, a New Zealand-born journalist turned town planner, who was organizing a lecture tour in 1914 of the main towns and cities of Australia and New Zealand on behalf of the London-based Garden Cities and Town Planning Association.[56] Reade and his co-lecturer, British architect William Davidge, were invited to Adelaide. The Australian leg of the Australasian Town Planning Tour of 1914–1915 commenced on 31 August 1914, not long after the outbreak of the Great War.[57]

Discussion of the impact and outcomes of the tour are beyond the temporal scope of this chapter. Suffice it to say that the tour sparked political, professional and community interest nationally and locally in town planning and in how to 'improve the appearance and utility of cities … and in bringing science and sense to bear upon the sprawling growth of prosaic and unlovely suburbs.'[58] Some seven decades since state-of-the-art ideas had informed the textbook colonial plan of Adelaide, South Australia's capital was on the cusp of receiving, and potentially adopting, the latest advances in modern town planning thought.

8

'No more loyal subjects'
Indians contesting White Australia

MARGARET ALLEN

From the last years of the nineteenth century and until the onset of the First World War, the determination of the Australian people and their government to make Australia a white man's country was firmly set in place. The new nation for the white 'race' was inaugurated 'in a radical act of racial exclusion'.[1] One of the earliest acts of the new federal parliament was the Immigration Restriction Act of 1901, which excluded 'aboriginal natives of Asia, Africa and the Pacific' from entry to Australia and saw the beginning of the steep decline in the numbers of people in Australia deemed to be prohibited immigrants under this act.

The Indian community in South Australia was relatively small at this time. It has been estimated that at Federation there were approximately 6000 Indians living in Australia. Palfreeman estimated that there were up to 7637 Indians in Australia during the first decade of the twentieth century, while Yarwood set the 1901 population at 4681, declining by 1911 to 3653 and by 1921 to 3150.[2] Thus it is likely that there were no more than 400 Indians in South Australia during the years leading up to the war. Most Indians in Australia were single men who travelled to Australia from the 1880s in search of fortune and adventure. Many came from the Punjab region, which had only recently succumbed to British rule. Sikhs and Muslims made up the majority of these immigrants. These men were often sojourners, staying a few years in Australia and then travelling back to India to spend time with family and indeed even to marry there and start a family, before returning for more years of work in Australia. Some spent up to 50 years following such circuits. While sojourning might have been a traditional pattern for workers from the Punjab, the hostility within the Australian community also played an important part in deterring Indian family life in Australia.

Many of these men worked as hawkers or merchants. Others set up stores, often in isolated or remote localities. The sugar industry in northern New South Wales and in Queensland attracted a large number of Indians. Here they often did the rough work of cane stripping, chipping and land clearing. The more successful among them were able to buy land and set themselves up as smallholders or farmers. During these years there were periodic rhetorical attacks upon Indians and public debates about whether they should be able to live and work in Australia. Hawkers were often seen as being a threat to white shopkeepers and also to women customers on isolated farms. It was alleged that they spread disease. Indeed, you could say that whereas in the 1880s the potential for Indians to prosper in Australia might have seemed promising, by the first decade of the twentieth century this was dwindling fast.

In this chapter I will look at the ways in which some Indians in South Australia addressed these issues and sought to make their way in the colony and the new nation. The chapter will examine the arguments they put, the alliances they made and the arenas in which they presented their views. It brings to light the agency and actions of individual Indians, who sought to make South Australia a more open and tolerant society. The chapter also brings forth evidence of organisations and alliances that brought together, in common cause, people from different ethnic communities adversely affected by the White Australia Policy. While they were ultimately unsuccessful in diverting policy from its deeply racialist foundations, their struggles inform our understandings of South Australia on the eve of the First World War, a war fought, ostensibly, 'to make the world safe for democracy' and for justice and freedom.

During the later nineteenth century, as efforts were being made to open up the Northern Territory, there were intense debates within the South Australian parliament and in the press about the importation of Indian labour to work in its northern climes. Indeed, the Northern Territory Immigration Act of 1882 did allow for the importation of such labour on a temporary basis. Although in fact no Indians were recruited to the Territory, it generated a certain amount of concern on the Labor side of politics. In 1891 the conservative John Langdon Parsons, who was very interested in the development of the Northern Territory, made another effort to get Indian labour, introducing an Indian Immigration Continuous Supply Bill.[3] This did not pass.

Opinion about what was termed 'coloured immigration' was divided between the conservative business side of politics, and the 'progressive' side and the labour movement. Through the press in 1900–1902 there was a slanging match between the conservative Parsons and the progressive Charles Cameron Kingston.[4] Kingston refuted the claims that Parsons, and also his son, H.A. Parsons, were supporters of White Australia. Instead he asserted that Parsons 'had strongly favoured Indian immigration'.[5] Parsons for his part defended himself, arguing that he had advocated and supported only the temporary immigration of Indians into the northern tropical areas of the Northern Territory, in a scheme similar to the indentured labour system, which saw over one million Indians working in tropical regions across the globe on a temporary basis.[6] Parsons argued that the temporary importation of Indian labour did not amount to a breach of the restricted immigration policy. He was of the belief that such areas 'could only be profitably cultivated by coloured labour'.[7] In his paper on 'The Northern Territory of South Australia', read before the Royal Geographical Society of South Australia in 1902, Parsons said that the 'Labor [*sic*] best adapted for Australian tropics ... are our fellow-subjects of the Indian Empire, especially the Tamils'.[8] An interesting aspect of this debate is that by the turn of the century, both sides of politics were endeavouring to present themselves as favouring White Australia.

Despite these efforts to introduce Indian workers, South Australia had a long history of seeking to limit or exclude Chinese and other 'coloured' immigrants.[9] Support for a total exclusion of 'coloured' workers gained support during the 1890s, and in 1896 the South Australian colonial parliament passed a Coloured Immigration Restriction Act. This legislation was disallowed by the governor and did not become law. However, in 1898 Kingston made further moves, introducing an Immigration Prohibition Bill, which also did not become law. With Federation, of course, the national Immigration Restriction Act of 1901 saw the principles of immigration restriction firmly established.

During the 1890s there was a certain amount of concern in South Australia about itinerant hawkers.[10] Racial prejudice and fears about economic competition were crucial to this social anxiety. In 1893 in South Australia the authorities refused to renew hawking licences of the Afghans, Assyrians and Chinese.[11]

Popular understandings tended to include all those seen as 'not white' in an inferior caste:

> With true British arrogance we virtually regard all such, whether Chinese, Afghans, Syrians, Hindus, or Persians, as the scum and offscouring of the earth. They have committed the unpardonable sin of being coloured, and although they were not consulted in the choice of their complexion they must perforce be Ishmaelites.[12]

In any event these hawkers were able to continue their rounds: in 1899 it was reported that almost all of the applicants for hawkers' licenses were approved. The applicants comprised 289 'Hindoos', 103 Syrians, 34 Chinese and 136 Europeans.[13]

Indian Hawkers at Mount Gambier, 1895. **[SLSA B 16740]**

These concerns about Indian hawkers surfaced from time to time, and there seemed to be an ongoing discussion of their worth. In 1905 a 'Country Schoolmistress' wrote to the *Register* in defence of Indian hawkers, suggesting that there should be some reciprocity within the British Empire:

> I … have always found them civil, honest, and obliging. I for one would be genuinely sorry if their licences were stopped … Considering many of our countrymen have made their fortunes in India, and that Calcutta owes its name, 'City of Palaces,' to the splendour of the British merchants' residences, is it fair to deny our Indian subjects the right to earn a decent living in our colonies?[14]

Bhagat Singh. **[*Critic*, 18 August 1909]**

In this chapter I focus particularly upon the efforts of Mr Bhagat Singh, an Adelaide merchant, to protest the discrimination to which the Indian and other 'Asiatic' communities were being subjected. While it is difficult to find out much about him, he does not seem to have been a hawker and was more educated and more able to move in European society than were some of the Indian hawkers. Bhagat Singh, pictured in one newspaper in three-piece suit with a watch chain, did not wear the turban and long hair of the traditional Sikh, which could mark him off from the majority society.[15] One reporter described him as a 'gentleman of wide culture and the broadest of views upon all subjects'.[16] He probably supplied the hawkers with their goods. Along with his shop in the city, he was also a manufacturer of underclothing and employed a number of women in his workshop. He had gone into business in Adelaide in c. 1894, and soon found that foreign merchants could be the butt of lawless violence. In 1899 he complained bitterly to the press about what happened after he held a man who had stolen from his Hindley Street shop. He claimed that 'hundreds of men and women tried to rescue this man from the police'. They were unsuccessful but proceeded to damage the shop, breaking the front window and stealing a tarpaulin. He asked whether:

> Indian natives [were] to be left unprotected, which would be wrong in any case, but is especially so, considering the great services they have rendered to the British Empire in the field of battle.[17]

Here he outlined the principles that underlay the protests of Indians (and of others), increasingly deemed to be *personae non gratae* in the Australian colonies. These were the rule of law, equality before the law, the importance of the British Empire and the respect owed to Indians due to their service in British forces.

With the passing of the Immigration Restriction Act in 1901, those already in Australia deemed to be 'Asiatics' could stay in Australia, although new immigrants who were described as 'aboriginal natives' from Asia, Africa and the Pacific were excluded. Those who had been in Australia for five years, who were of good character and who had assets in Australia of around £200 were regarded as domiciled in Australia and if they chose to travel abroad could return to Australia. Those who were not aware of the implications of the legislation or who had little capital were less fortunate.[18] Theoretically their ability to carry on their work in Australia was not affected.

Nihal Singh, Indian hawker, and his team, Terowie, 1911. **[SLSA B 32952]**

In 1904, however, a Licensed Hawkers' Bill was introduced to the South Australian Parliament. The intention was to deny hawkers' licenses to those of Indian, Syrian, Chinese and Afghan backgrounds. Such a measure struck at the livelihoods of those from these backgrounds who had been plying their trade for many years and also at the livelihood of merchants such as Bhagat Singh, who supplied hawkers with goods to sell in rural areas. The measure also moved beyond the exclusion of further Indians and other 'Asiatics' from coming to Australia – it amounted to an attack on the ability of Indians, Syrians, Chinese and Afghans already resident in Australia to earn their living. It was similar to legislation being proposed or passed in other states. Thus the 1904 Factory Act in Western Australia limited the working hours of 'Asiatics' and was framed to include workshops where only one person worked. It mentioned laundries explicitly, particularly targeting Chinese workers, even those who worked from their own homes. [19]

Late in 1904, Bhagat Singh wrote to the press asking that the public give 'thorough consideration' to the proposed Bill. He pointed out that it was discriminatory, because it would make 'two laws for the subjects of one Power, applying especially to Indians, who are British subjects just the same as Australians'.[20] Taking a view across the British Empire, he emphasised what he saw as the extraordinary nature of the proposed legislation: 'Two laws are not known to be in force for the same subjects in the British dominions'. Making a deft reference to white and Christian notions of their own inherent superiority, he contended that it was brutal, selfish, uncivilised and unchristian to allow people to live in Australia and then to remove 'the only means of their living'. He pointed out the economic benefits to the community of the hawkers and Indian and Syrian manufacturers, noting that the public could buy from 'the cheapest man' and that the 'scores of girls employed by Indian and Syrian merchants for manufacturing purposes' would lose their jobs if the Bill was enacted. He reminded the readers that Indian soldiers had 'shed their blood to protect British interests', and thus 'our gracious King's Indian subjects' were 'entitled to be ruled under one law' and not to be subject to discriminatory legislation. He contended that the unity of British subjects was important, and thus 'all the British dominions should be united' in order 'to protect and uphold the honor of the British flag'. He referred not only to past battles in which Indians had fought for the British but prophetically struck a warning about the future, hoping that circumstances would not arise that would require 'Indian British subjects ... to stand by the side of Australians, and shed their blood to keep the honor [*sic*] of the British flag'.[21]

Clearly these hawkers and merchants were very troubled by this Bill, and before it was debated, Chinese, Indians and Syrians joined together to fight it and other such legislation. In September 1905 they formed the United Asiatic League. This is significant, as previously there does not seem to have been any united action by these communities against the White Australia Policy. Bhagat Singh presided at the meeting of about 200 at the City Mission Hall in Light Square. The view was that united action was finally necessary. They:

> had hitherto been content to submit quietly to pinpricks of various kinds, but a feeling had arisen that their interests would be better safe guarded if the various sections were to unite in a league for the purpose.[22]

Bhagat Singh became president, supported by Gee Wah, from the Chinese community, as secretary and Assaf Habib, a Syrian, as treasurer. They planned to organise a voting bloc, getting their members onto the electoral rolls and sponsoring a national movement. The League's objects were:

> to protect the interests of Asiatics and their descendants in any existing or proposed Federal or State legislation, and to secure

> and preserve for them civil rights and privileges equal to those enjoyed by British subjects.[23]

They argued that their members, who had invested in property and plant, would be adversely affected by the proposed Hawkers' Bill, which would also inconvenience residents in outlying parts of the state who depended upon their service. They believed the Bill 'detrimental to the interest of the British Empire, and opposed to the well-founded boast of justice and equality to all British subjects'.[24]

Clearly the League had influential friends. A League petition against the Bill was presented to the House of Assembly by Mr Lewis Cohen MP. Cohen had been a successful businessman in Sydney and Fiji before settling in Adelaide. He was a leading citizen, having been mayor of Adelaide a number of times since 1889, and later becoming Lord Mayor of Adelaide.[25] He opposed the Bill on the grounds of British justice, but his own religious and ethnic background also had some bearing. He was British born but Jewish and made a comparison between the proposed treatment of these hawkers and 'the persecution of the Jews in Russia'.[26] Eric Richards has argued that Cohen was opposed to coloured immigration.[27] Nevertheless, he stonewalled the Hawkers' Bill and it did not pass. In the course of the parliamentary debate he asked:

> Should I seek to do an injustice to a man simply because his color [*sic*] is a little darker than my own?[28]

All three leaders of the United Asiatic League were well able to move in Australian society. Apart from Bhagat Singh, George Gee Wah was Australian born and a Christian. He had come to South Australia from Victoria to train for the China Mission, but stayed in South Australia working as a missioner among the Chinese community in Adelaide on behalf of the Adelaide City Mission.[29] Assaf Habib, a Syrian, was a businessman in Waymouth Street, Adelaide.

All three communities that made up the League had suffered from racist attacks. The Coory family were leading members of the Syrian community, and Tanus Coory and his young relative, Joseph Regis Coory, were reported to be moving spirits behind the League.[30] Joseph Coory was born near Beirut but came to Australia as a small child. He attended Christian Brothers College in Adelaide before beginning law studies at the University of Adelaide. He did not complete the degree but went into business. He was an enthusiastic leader in the Boy Scout movement, gaining the position of Chief Scout Commissioner for Australia when only in his twenties. He was very patriotic and sought to enlist for the Boer War, even though he was only sixteen years old at the time.[31]

The Coory family were well used to having to defend themselves and others from racist attacks. They had taken up the cause of 'Asiatics', in particular those from Asia Minor, when there was an outcry about them in the community in 1893. The Coory Brothers questioned the notion of 'Australia for Australians', asking in a letter to the *Register* 'Who are Australians? Every settler is surely entitled to that denomination'. The denial of naturalisation to Asiatics was clearly rankling. After listing the contributions of the Chinese, Hindus, Sikhs and Afghans to the community, the brothers turned to the Syrians. It was, they asserted, an arbitrary geographical line that placed Syria in Asia. They were Christian, 'sober, industrious, honest, thrifty [and] law-abiding'. They were criticised for being traders, but asserted that many of their compatriots had turned from other occupations to commerce because, as they noted sarcastically, 'the fearless, independent, fairplay loving, superior Australian tabooes them'.[32] Their letter prompted someone, using the name 'James Swift', to issue a series of accusations against Asiatics, alleging that the Syrians were a 'dirty race of people' and that the Coory brothers could 'scarcely write English'.[33] In their response the brothers noted their English was improving, but that they could write letters in Arabic, which they doubted Swift could do, and that within their household they had 'the command of seven languages'.[34]

The United Asiatic League took up the opportunity of the visit of the Chinese Commissioner, His Excellency the Prefect Hwang Hon Cheng, to Australia in 1906 to air their concerns about the treatment of Asiatics with the British Government. The Commissioner had been sent by the Chinese Government to inquire into the situation of Chinese living in Australia. Bhagat Singh handed over an address from the League to the Commissioner. At a lunch for the Commissioner at the York Hotel, Bhagat Singh spoke of the confidence the Asiatics had in Great Britain. Referring at length to the Immigration Restriction Act, which he described as 'most unjust', Bhagat Singh made the point that:

> They were a peaceful and well-behaved people, yet they were being treated as though they were not good enough for Australia. The people of India and Afghanistan were undoubtedly loyal to the British throne, yet arrivals from hostile countries were preferred to them.[35]

On behalf of the League, he asked that the Commissioner 'use his influence with the Home Government to have the alien, immigration laws of the Commonwealth modified'.[36] The legislation was not modified. The Indian and Chinese communities in particular continued to decline as many of those who left the country were unable to return.

Bhagat Singh continued to enjoy the support of many in the business community. Indeed, in December 1908 he was initiated into the Royal Antediluvian Order of Buffaloes (RAOB). He gave a dinner to celebrate, and Joseph Coory proposed a toast to his health. Bhagat Singh then made a toast to the 'Commercial men', complimenting them on their high standards and describing them as 'cordial in their relations towards Asiatics'. Once more he referred to the record of the Indians, and particularly of the Sikhs, in the British forces. He emphasised the way that Australians benefitted from their service: 'This help given to the British Empire by India really benefited Australia, a part of the Empire.'[37] Considering the service of Indian soldiers, he believed that 'the treatment meted out to them in some directions could be improved'.[38]

Bhagat Singh advanced quickly within the RAOB, for late in 1909 he became the chair of the Adelaide lodge.[39] He joined a new branch at suburban Marryatville. On the eve of his departure for India in 1912, the members made a presentation to him. He had earned their esteem being a Past Primo and a Knight of Merit, positions of note within the Buffaloes. Those present hoped that the illuminated address would 'bring back many pleasant memories of evenings spent with the Marryatville brethren'.[40]

While these fellow lodge members expressed their affection and esteem for Bhagat Singh, he was under no illusions as regards the general situation of Indians and other 'Asiatics' in Australia. He and other members of the United Asiatic League were 'not personally hopeful of much amelioration of the lot of Asiatics in Australia'. Bhagat Singh believed the situation was so bad 'that the treatment meted out to them cannot possibly get worse'.[41] They had 'No time for the Labor Party!', believing it to be the source of their troubles. League members made it clear that they did not advocate 'unlimited immigration' but rather 'fair play for those of us already here, and a decent system of selection of candidates for entrance, but an equality with other races'.[42] Looking forward, Bhagat Singh saw that it would be a long struggle to gain equality in Australia. Indeed, he countered:

> When India obtains home rule, as she inevitably must, the lot of Asiatics all over the world will be bettered by the respect which will naturally be given them.[43]

During the period before the outbreak of the First World War, Indians and other 'Asiatics' found their rights and opportunities shrinking within a determinedly White Australia. In their protests, Indians made alliances with all groups adversely affected by the restrictive immigration regime. They put forward arguments about their contributions to the South Australian community, their loyalty to the British Empire, their position as British subjects, and Indian contributions to the British Empire by way of military service. While all these arguments may have stopped some aspects of anti-Asiatic legislation, generally their efforts were ineffective.

Bhagat Singh had hinted darkly about an impending conflict in which Indian servicemen would be needed to protect Australian freedoms. Indeed, in the First Word War thousands of Indians served in British forces and many gave their lives. Indians in South Australia also served within the Australian forces and Sarn Singh, a farmer from Maggea in the Murray Mallee, died on the Western Front defending Australia.[44] Although in the post-war period the British Government sought to influence the

Australian government to treat Indians in Australia better, there was really little improvement in their position. As the number of Indians resident in Australia declined during the inter-war years, they did not cease to protest, albeit intermittently, against the restrictive and discriminatory legislation. As Bhagat Singh had predicted, it was only after India became independent that Australian restrictive legislation was finally removed.

9

German South Australia on the eve of war

PETER MONTEATH

On the eve of the First World War, South Australia was the most German of the Australian states. German South Australians and their British 'cousins' could look back on decades of collaborative endeavour based on mutual respect, if not admiration. Yet within days of the outbreak of the war, German South Australians throughout the state would be subjected to openly proclaimed charges of treachery. Within months, some of them found themselves behind barbed wire in the 'concentration camp' established on Torrens Island.[1] And before the war had ended, German place names would be expunged from the map of South Australia, German-language publications banned, and German schools closed.

How did it come to this in such a short time? What were the dynamics, cloaked by a history of apparent harmony, which led to such an outcome? This essay prods at the history of the German presence in South Australia in search of signs that perhaps not all was as it seemed. It looks for answers in the history of German settlement over several decades and in the evolving relationships of German Australians with their European homelands. But it also looks beyond the German communities to consider the attitudes of others toward Germans, and how by the early twentieth century those attitudes were moulded by growing international tensions and nascent Australian nationalism.

Germans in South Australia

The founding myth of the German presence in South Australia concerns the so-called 'Old Lutherans', who settled in the colony to escape religious persecution in their native Prussia. The Prussian king had obliged the subjects in his realm to adopt the liturgy of the unified state church he had created. This was anathema to many, including the Old Lutheran pastors, who were reluctant to abandon their traditional services in favour of the new liturgy dictated from above. In effect the pastors were civil servants and had little room for manoeuvre. At best they might meet privately with their congregations, but even then they risked state persecution. Rather than express open resistance against the state, many of those pastors pursued the option of emigrating from Prussia. While some contemplated Russia or the Americas as their destination, a happy confluence of circumstances rendered possible immigration to Australia. Just as Pastor August Kavel, of Klemzig in Prussia's Brandenburg, sought a new home for his flock, George Fife Angas, of the South Australia Company in London, sought rural labour to ensure the viability of the colony to be established in the Antipodes.[2]

Kavel's people were not the first Germans to arrive in the colony. A handful had been present aboard the very first vessels charged with founding a settlement, but Kavel's was the first substantial group, and it set a trend to be followed for several years. After Kavel, other pastors guided their congregations to South Australia, typically using Adelaide as a stepping stone before establishing communities to the east in the Adelaide Hills and, eventually, beyond.

The reasons for the durability of this narrative are obvious enough. For the descendants of those first Lutherans, the story is testament to the doctrinal purity and principled resistance of their forebears. It records and transmits the multiple hardships the Old Lutherans endured in leaving their homeland, making a perilous journey over many months, and then confronting and overcoming the challenges posed by the new and strange land in which they found themselves. For other South Australians, the tale of the Old Lutherans confirms that the state's origins lay in a 'paradise of dissent', where people were judged not by their religious beliefs but by their strength of character and commitment to shared colonial endeavour.[3]

Enduring and influential though the story is, in reality it is not representative of the wider experience of German immigration to South Australia. Friedrich Wilhelm III, the Prussian king who had sought to impose a unified church and liturgy on his subjects, died in 1840. With his demise the compulsion to use the new liturgy disappeared. That is not to say that the emigration of Old Lutherans ceased overnight. Fears of renewed persecution persisted, and encouraging communications home from co-religionists in South Australia persuaded others to make the voyage. Increasingly, however, the primary motivation for emigration through the 1840s was not religious but economic. The privations of life on the land in mid-nineteenth-century Prussia, and in other German states as well, convinced many to try their luck in South Australia. A flurry of guides for potential German immigrants to the colony published from the late 1840s gave them appropriate information and advice on how they might establish new lives there.[4]

Unsurprisingly, those who had come from rural backgrounds in one of the German states tended to make their way to the rural

German communities in South Australia. In these communities they found much that was reminiscent of home. The German farmers, unlike their British counterparts, devoted their labours to a variety of farming activities rather than the cultivation of a single cash crop – a practice that would help them through the lean years that inevitably came. The Lutheran Church occupied the central place not just in the religious but also in the social life of the communities. With its heavy emphasis on an understanding of the 'word of God', the Lutheran Church promoted the maintenance of the German language and of both the secular and religious uses to which it was put.

The extent to which these rural German communities were able to recreate the cultural milieu of their homelands is beautifully expressed in the writings of Friedrich Gerstäcker. The most popular and prolific German travel writer of his time, Gerstäcker made his way to South Australia in 1851, determined to witness how his countrymen had adapted to life in a new environment. Visiting a German house in the Barossa in that year, Gerstäcker observed with a sense of wonderment:

> I knew well enough already, from the United States, how my countrymen like to carry with them what they can possibly bring on board of a vessel, and some are really sorry at being obliged to leave houses and stables; but I could never have thought it possible, without seeing it here, how they had been able to transplant their old rooms from home, with everything that belonged to them originally, even the smell, to such a far-off and strange country as Australia. Not only their dress was the same – there was an excuse for that – but the tables and chairs, the stoves, the glass panes in the windows, the nails in the wall, the kettles, and pans, and pannikins, ay, even the earthen

> plates and dishes, with verses of Scripture or Catechism written upon them, and glazed over in the beautiful hand-writing of the potter. If they had taken at home one of these rooms out, packed it up carefully in cotton, and planted it again in the New World, they could not have preserved it better.[5]

Yet Gerstäcker, on the strength of his own observations in South Australia – including a couple of visits to Adelaide – was well aware that not all Germans had sought to recreate their homeland. While the appeal of the land remained strong, there were other considerations, both 'push' and 'pull' factors, which shaped the course of German migration to South Australia.

There were those, for example, who wanted to pursue their trades in a country that might value their skills and talents more than their German homelands did at that time. Some, such as the miners from the Harz district of Hanover, who came to work in the fledgling mining industry in South Australia – an industry that was securing for the province a more stable economic footing – responded to quite specific needs in the young country.

Others came for political reasons. After the failure of Europe's democratic revolutions of 1848–1849, there were many disillusioned German liberals who sought not only to escape the threat of vengeful persecution at home, but to play their part in what appeared the politically progressive context of Britain's bold South Australian experiment. Many such men and women of liberal persuasion were Berliners who boarded the *Princess Louise*, a vessel that berthed in Port Adelaide in August 1849. Sooner or later, some of the entries on that vessel's passenger list – Schomburgk, Mücke, Bühring, Schramm, Linger, Basedow and others – would become household names in the colony.

All of this meant that there was a much greater variety in the German presence in South Australia than is often acknowledged. This was especially true of Adelaide, where a significant minority of Germans chose to live. It was not only that the urban Germans distinguished themselves from the rural communities through their greater willingness to assimilate by speaking English and assuming places in an overwhelmingly 'British' host society, but that the urban population was additionally diverse. While the majority were Lutherans, there were others who were Catholics or even Jews; some expressed their assimilation by turning to the Church of England. There were unskilled Germans who contributed to the ranks of the urban working class, as well as tradesmen and craftsmen of humble social standing. But then there were also Germans of solidly patrician status – doctors, lawyers and merchants – who became the proverbial pillars of Adelaide society, wielding influence in the realms of finance and politics.

So great were the differences among the Germans in South Australia that they led in some circumstances to antagonism, if not hostility. That was true even of the Old Lutherans. Kavel's role as undisputed leader of the community was soon challenged by another pastor, Gottlieb Daniel Fritzsche, who arrived from Posen with his congregation in October of 1841. By the following year this congregation had founded settlements at Bethanien in the Barossa Valley and Lobethal in the Adelaide Hills.[6] Within five years it was evident that differences existed between Fritzsche's beliefs and those of Kavel, differences so severe as to cause the Old Lutherans to split into groups. These doctrinal differences, along with the institutional split into two rival synods, were not healed for well over a century.[7]

Similarly in Adelaide differences opened over the issue of

what kind of German cultural legacy might be cultivated at the German Club. Founded in 1854, the original German Club catered to the interests of middle-class Germans, who while following the path of assimilation also wished to preserve German high culture. Increasing numbers of Germans of more modest social standing by contrast had different expectations of their club. By the last two decades of the century, working-class Germans had even introduced socialist ideas into the community and the club. So deep were the divisions that in 1886 an alternative association was set up in opposition to the club: this was the South Australian General German Association (*Südaustralischer Allgemeiner Deutscher Verband*, SAADV). The association's brief was to cater to the needs and wishes of workers, so that it in time came to be viewed by members of the German Club as a 'den of communism'.[8]

Members of the South Australian German Association in Adelaide on the eve of war, 1914. [History SA, SAGPC GN 05182]

The loyalty question

It would be misleading to suggest that the issue of the loyalty of South Australia's German population was never raised during the years when they made their indelible mark on the young colony's development. Whether the Germans made serious efforts to assimilate or whether, as generally in country areas, they tended to cultivate German language and culture in closed communities, suspicions were occasionally voiced that the Germans' intention was to remain a power unto themselves. In an expression of a milder form of anxiety, British South Australians wondered whether the very existence of a substantial German population might by itself dilute and thereby degrade the colony's British heritage.

In 1857 the German newspaper editor Rudolf Reimer felt the need to put all such fears to rest. Targeting the British readers of the *Adelaide Observer*, he sought to make it plain that the Germans were not seeking to establish a state within a state, or an *imperium in imperio*, as the favoured Latin phrase put it. Reimer wrote that he wished to 'forestall any possible imputation of seeking to foster a spirit of isolated nationality amongst my fellow countrymen'.[9] Later the same year the *Adelaide Times* assured its readers:

> We have no fear that our nationality will depart from us or that John Bull will bid adieu to South Australia because a few of his German cousins may have arrived on a permanent visit … The colony is and ever will be essentially a British land.[10]

The dominant view through much of the nineteenth century, among Germans and British alike, was that the values and traditions that many Germans chose to uphold were a matter for them and for them alone. Most British people in the colony, as Ian Harmstorf concludes, 'lived undismayed with the German sub-culture in their midst'.[11]

There were historical reasons in South Australia why suspicions of German disloyalty were voiced only rarely, did not gain traction and were quickly quelled. In contrast to other states, the heyday of German immigration was in the first fifteen years of the colony's existence. By 1854 almost half of the Germans to come to South Australia before World War I had already arrived.[12] The discovery of gold in Victoria and New South Wales meant not only that the focus of German migration to Australia shifted east; it also prompted internal migration away from South Australia. That is not to say that from that time the German presence in South Australia diminished – indeed by the end of century some 10 per cent of the colony's population were either German-born or were of German descent.[13] But because so much of the German immigration had occurred early in the colony's history, by the end of the century the number of those of German descent outnumbered the German-born South Australians by more than two to one.[14]

This pattern of German settlement in South Australia – heavy early, easing in the second half of the century – had implications for any assessment of the Germans' loyalties. It meant that the majority of Germans and German descendants living in rural areas, steeped as they were in Lutheranism, were inclined to accept the political authority of the state. They stood in a tradition that stretched back via Martin Luther to the Biblical dictum that one should 'Render unto Caesar the things that are Caesar's, and unto God the things that are God's'.[15] It was not the role of the subject or citizen to call into question secular authority. The exception would be in circumstances where the state acted in such a way as to interfere in God's kingdom. Such a

Emmeline Bayer, granddaughter of the prominent German doctor Friedrich Carl Bayer, shows her colours in 1887. [SLSA B 7723 23]

breach of the separation of the two kingdoms, in the view of the Old Lutherans, had occurred with the Prussian king's efforts to create a unified state church and impose a new liturgy. Even in those circumstances, the response of the Old Lutherans was not to rebel against the state, but rather to remove themselves from its boundaries through emigration. Their ready acquiescence in the power of the colony of South Australia earned them respect and praise and contributed to their reputation as model settlers. As early as 1839 the *Southern Australian* newspaper observed of the Germans, 'The male peasant raises his hat as he passes you ... our labouring fellow countrymen ... may well learn one or two valuable lessons'.[16]

The distinctive pattern of German migration to South Australia also meant that most South Australian Germans had not experienced German unification in 1871. When most migrated there was no unified Germany, just a patchwork of states. In many cases their immigration to Australia was an indication that they felt no strong identification with their homeland; there were, after all, compelling reasons to have left it behind. Their primary loyalties shifted to the place that had accepted them – to South Australia. Insofar as they retained loyalties to their homelands at all, they were at best regional loyalties, based in a sense of culture and place rather than political allegiance. As for their bonds with their adoptive homeland, arguably the German settlers were the most devoted of South Australians, precisely because their allegiances were undivided. British South Australians, in contrast, were inclined to view South Australia as an extension of their British homeland; their primary loyalties were to Queen and Empire.

The German affirmation of loyalty to South Australia was a familiar refrain through the full course of the colonial period. As early as 1839 the famed German geologist and early immigrant to South Australia Johann Menge had implored his fellow settlers, 'we shall all become Australians'.[17] Decades later, in 1896, but in exactly the same spirit, Carl Krichauff had intoned in the *Australische Zeitung*, 'True Germans ... are always highly patriotic South Australians.'[18]

The age of imperial rivalries

Through the middle of the nineteenth century, relations between the British Empire and the German states were consistently cordial. That applied at the level of high politics and inter-state relations, but it played out also in the towns and villages of South Australia as much as in the capitals of Europe.

At the time of South Australia's founding, William IV was king not only of the United Kingdom and Ireland but also of Hanover. He had married a German, Princess Adelheid of Saxe-Meiningen, who duly became Queen Adelaide and gave her name to the capital of the colony. In 1837 William was succeeded by his young niece Victoria, who had been raised by her German-born mother and in 1840 married her first cousin, Prince Albert of Saxe-Coburg and Gotha. Albert died in 1861, but his Germanophile widow Victoria remained on the throne until 1901.

Nonetheless it is true that the tenor of Anglo-German relations changed after the creation of a united Germany in 1871. Unification had been achieved through a series of wars, the results of which confirmed the potency of the new Germany created through Prussian military might. A single, united Germany changed the balance of European politics, as unification Chancellor Otto von Bismarck demanded a German place at the table of the Great Powers.

The challenge to Britain became all the greater in the following decade, when Germany followed the path of establishing itself as a colonial power. Albeit reluctantly, Bismarck followed what appeared the logic of the age and committed Germany to the European scramble for colonies in Africa, Asia and the Pacific, where, as a latecomer to colonisation, the Germans ruffled the feathers of established colonial powers like Britain.

In trade and commerce, too, Germany emerged in Europe and across the globe as a powerhouse. Long-established British interests appeared threatened by ambitious German newcomers, eager to claim their share of sources of raw materials, places to invest capital, and markets for an economy industrialising at unprecedented speed.

Australia could not be isolated from these developments. In the late nineteenth century, and even into the first decade at least of the twentieth, Australians continued to identify heavily with Britain and British interests. The challenges posed by an emergent Germany did not go unnoticed, and the mood of British suspicion of German motives spread throughout the empire. In distant South Australia there were occasional signs that attitudes toward Germans and Australians of German descent were changing.

One example of the frostier climate with which Germans had to contend in the last decade of the century was provided by the zoologist Amandus Zietz, the assistant director of the South Australian Museum. Zietz was one of a long and illustrious line of German scientists in Adelaide, but in an 1897 letter to an old friend, J.D.E. Schmeltz of the Ethnographic Museum in Leiden, Zietz lamented, 'Being a German is becoming a disadvantage here.' There was, he complained, 'political friction between the land of our birth and England, to which I have to swear an oath of allegiance'.[19]

The situation did not improve with the outbreak of the Boer War, to which South Australia, like the other Australian colonies, sent a contingent. The Kaiser's professed sympathies with the Boers triggered the expression of renewed doubts about the loyalties of South Australia's Germans. Friedrich Basedow, the editor of the *Australische Zeitung*, expressed his dismay that German South Australians like himself could not openly criticise the war without drawing accusations of treachery, while those of British descent need hold no such fears. The reason, he surmised, was that 'we, although citizens, with equal rights, are Germans (helots?) and therefore must "down boy" (as to a dog)'.[20]

These suspicions were not allayed by the efforts of German officialdom to promote *Deutschtum* (Germanness) in those parts of the world where Germany had a formal diplomatic presence. It was the task of Germany's representatives in all parts of the globe to promote Germany's interests and to cultivate German language and culture. In Australia's case, this *Deutschtumspolitik*, the policy of promoting Germanness, was driven largely by the consul general in Sydney, aided by the efforts of honorary consuls in various parts of the country and occasional visits undertaken by high-ranking naval officers. The most visible manifestation of the official cultivation of *Deutschtum* in Australia was the annual *Nationalfest* (national festival), staged in Sydney every January to commemorate the anniversary of German unification.[21] The spirit of these events was captured by a witness in 1906:

> To all excitement is suddenly added the sound of gunfire, 'spread out' is the order given. We can hardly step aside before a group of navy youngsters storms in, dressed in white, flattering suits – with guns, at the double, march, march – they pass us. A pretty sight these young fellows, sons of German countrymen, which greatly add to the festival with their 'military' performance.[22]

In its conception, *Deutschtumspolitik* in Australia was not meant to pose a challenge to German Australians' loyalty to their country or indeed to the British Empire. Its express goal was an apolitical one – the promotion of culture. To its critics, however, especially those who noted martial undertones in its application, the promotion of culture was not so easily separated from politics. *Deutschtumspolitik* represented a threat that had to be countered.

The German Consul, Dr Irmer, and a welcoming party in Hahndorf in 1907. The house in the background belonged to Alfred Von Doussa. [SLSA B 30468]

There were inevitable reverberations of these tensions in South Australia, yet expressions of pride in the unified Germany were relatively muted here. For South Australian Germans, the unification of Germany, while noteworthy, was a matter of some ambivalence, for many even of indifference. As Ian Harmstorf points out, of the approximately 18,000 Germans who came to South Australia to the year 1900, 75 per cent had arrived before the unification of Germany.[23] For the longer-established majority, most of whom lived in rural areas, the question of loyalty to South Australia was not raised – at least not by them. The greater impact was among those who had arrived in South Australia after unification, and who were more likely to remain in Adelaide than to settle in rural areas. For urban Germans, unification was much more likely to be viewed as 'a fulfilment of a great historical drama'.[24] And even among this group, there was no guarantee that they shared the patriotic fervour of the German visitors promoting *Deutschtumspolitik*. When the officers and crew of a visiting naval vessel visited the SAADV, they were surprised to find that the venue was festooned not with images of the Kaiser, but of leading socialists.[25]

The eve of war

To the casual visitor to South Australia on the eve of war, the German presence was as visible as it had been for decades. In the city of Adelaide German businesses offered all manner of services and products to Germans and non-Germans alike. At the western end of Rundle Street was Beehive Corner, premises of the German confectioner Carl Stratmann. Heading east down Rundle Street, the visitor would encounter a number of German businesses, among them Café Kindermann, where they might stop for a pastry named 'Berliner Pfannkuchen', or simply 'Berliner'. Thirsts could be quenched with beers served at German hotels such as the King of Hanover and the Hamburg Hotel, or with coffee at one of the German coffee shops.

From the eastern end of Rundle Street, it was a mere hop to the Botanical Garden, which owed a huge debt to its former director, the German Richard Schomburgk. It was Schomburgk who was responsible for the elegant glass Palm House, fully imported from Bremen and assembled on site piece-by-piece in 1877. Other North Terrace institutions, too, relied heavily on the talents and hard work of their German employees. For years the German language was spoken in many parts of the city's museum and its university. The state's parliament, too, had many German-speaking representatives over the decades. On the eve of war, the state's attorney-general was Robert Homburg, who had made quite a reputation for himself through his legal practice.

To the south of Rundle Street was Adelaide's German Quarter. In this district could be found such 'German' institutions as the premises of the SAADV and the Menz Biscuit Factory, along with pubs of a distinctively German character such as the Tivoli, where German farmers gathered on town visits. Three German churches – Bethlehem Church, located on the corner of Flinders Street and Sudholz Place, the Trinity Lutheran Church on Angas Street, and St Stephen's on Wakefield Street – imposed their presence on the urban streetscape. East of the city centre was the suburb of Klemzig, named for one of the Brandenburg villages left behind by some of the earliest of German settlers.

Similarly in rural South Australia, where the majority of German South Australians still lived, the signs of a German past and present were not easily missed. The German place names – Hahndorf, Lobethal, Blumberg, Kaiserstuhl, Langmeil, Bethanien and many others – dotted the regions of the Adelaide Hills and the Barossa Valley and testified to the pioneering efforts of the earliest German settlers. Churches, farmhouses and barns built by Germans in faithfully German styles bespoke an enduring German presence, while German-born farmers and their descendants tended the variety of crops they had planted and cultivated successfully over the decades. In the early twentieth century they remained by and large the model settlers they had proved themselves to be over many decades, living in productive harmony with their British neighbours.

Yet appearances deceived. While South Australia, like other states, was subjected to efforts to maintain and promote German culture, the truth was that by the beginning of the twentieth century *Deutschtum* was in a state of decline. So adept had Germans been at assimilating into an overwhelming British society, that German culture and language were undergoing what appeared on closer inspection to be a terminal contraction.

This is evident, for example, in Theodor Hebart's assertion that when he arrived in South Australia in 1902, young people had to be constantly reminded to speak German when they were not by themselves. As a pastor he had a particular interest in the maintenance of the German language, since, like many Lutherans, Hebart attached great importance to the German language as the vehicle through which God's word was best expressed. Hebart believed that the Lutheran Church had actively contributed to the maintenance of the German language among the first generation of German South Australians born outside Germany. The next generation, however, in Hebart's view had little or no desire to uphold either the German language or customs.[26] The process appeared to be one of inexorable anglicisation, no matter what the Lutheran pastors and the proponents of *Deutschtumspolitik* might have wished for. And in South Australia, with its history of early German migration, the original, German-speaking group found themselves in a dwindling minority.

One of those proponents of *Deutschtumspolitik* was a visitor to South Australia in 1912, just a before the outbreak of war. It was the German diplomat Richard Kiliani, who, after his appointment as consul general in Sydney, undertook to travel widely and report on the conditions of Germans and of German culture in Australia.

Kiliani's impressions of South Australia left him in no doubt as to the challenges confronting any pursuit of *Deutschtumspolitik*. He observed that '*Deutschtum* was slowly disappearing, in the city faster than in the country where one found close communities. But nevertheless it was happening continuously and everywhere'. His analysis of the situation led him to conclude that the main reason for the erosion of *Deutschtum* was above all the education of German children in Australian schools. Other explanations were to be found in the trend toward intermarriage outside the German communities and the slowing pace of immigration from Germany.[27]

What was most disturbing for Kiliani, however, was the extent to which erosion of *Deutschtum* was even proceeding apace in the rural areas. He observed:

> The people of German descent like the others in South Australia seem incapable of organising themselves politically to take German goods or even for their own advantage. Their political ambitions when they exist were only to take part in the Australian political scene. The thinly distributed population no doubt accounts for the fact that at the moment and indeed into the foreseeable future voters both Australian and German seem to be interested only in their own districts.[28]

For Kiliani these trends were a cause of deep regret. He argued for the continuation of efforts to keep *Deutschtum* alive, for example through donations of old books and Bibles to churches and schools. But his overall assessment was hard-headed and pessimistic. The German way of doing things was 'being swallowed up by the Anglo-Saxon way of doing things, particularly as in this case it is by the superficial Australian way'.[29] And while the Lutheran church might once have provided a valuable agent in the promotion of *Deutschtum*, this was no longer the case. The Church, Kiliani noted, was struggling to attract the numbers it had known in the previous century; in the hope of reversing the trend, growing numbers of pastors were now preaching in English.[30]

A later report, dated April 1913, could offer no comfort that the situation was improving. On the contrary, Kiliani observed grimly:

> The German church and schools in South Australia stand more or less in a state of collapse. The Lutheran Church has the highest loss rate of any church according to official government statistics, and this tendency has increased from decade to decade ... in twenty-five years there would be only a small rump of the Lutheran Church and that would be speaking English. The experience has been that Germans who left the church turned their backs on *Deutschtum*.[31]

In the realm of politics, things were no more encouraging. At a public welcome in Tanunda, Kiliani was assured by his hosts that they remained doggedly committed to cultivating their German heritage; but, as the local pastor made clear in his address, this was not to be confused with political loyalty to the German state:

> He said they welcomed Herr Kiliani as the representative of the fatherland. They did so from a sense of filial regard and thankfulness to the land whence their ancestors came. Their object was not the maintenance of a connection with the fatherland in the sense of German patriotism. The links that bound them to the old home were something more ideal,

> namely spiritual good. They were striving to maintain German spirituality, German customs and habits, and to inculcate these in the coming generation. Nevertheless, they would strive to be faithful subjects to their new home.[32]

That is not to say that there were no representatives of communities in South Australia who clung tenaciously to German language and culture, but they were by now an exception rather than the rule, and they provided no solid foundation on which a vigorous *Deutschtumspolitik* could be built.

Tellingly, the German consul in Adelaide at that time was not one of those rare exceptions. Kiliani could hardly fail to notice that Hugo Carl Emil Muecke, like so many German South Australians by the early twentieth century, was heavily assimilated. Kiliani noted that Muecke's house was run 'like that of an Englishman'; he even wondered whether, to set an example, Muecke might be replaced as consul.[33]

Kiliani's observations were undoubtedly accurate. Not just in his official capacity as consul, but in the trajectory of his life story, Muecke represented Adelaide's German community. Having arrived in Adelaide as a seven-year-old in 1849, Muecke mixed successfully in the English-speaking commercial world, became naturalised, converted to Anglicanism, married an Englishwoman, served on numerous boards and in the Legislative Council, was a member of both the Adelaide Club and the German Club, and in the year following Kiliani's visit became chairman of BHP.[34] Like many fellow businessmen of German birth or descent, Muecke had embedded his commercial and social life very firmly in the world of Anglo-Australian Adelaide. He represented the views of many when he said:

> To remain strong genuine Germans, that means to treasure the richness of the German language, the language of poets and thinkers, as well as German customs and good habits, but at the same time to remain faithful to the English king.[35]

Conclusion

With the outbreak of war in August 1914, the loyalty of German South Australians would be questioned once more. The issue had been raised many times before, from the early days of German settlement through to the age of a unified Germany and Anglo-German imperial rivalry. And when it had been raised, it had always been answered – from within the German community and indeed outside it – in the same way. That is, although German South Australians maintained an attachment to German culture, language and traditions – albeit an increasingly tenuous one – they did not feel a patriotic devotion to any German state. This was as true of the Old Lutherans, who deliberately severed the ties with the state that persecuted them back in the 1830s, as it was of German South Australians in the early twentieth century. The irony of the breakdown of relations between German and British South Australians from August 1914 was that it occurred just at the point when the Germans were more firmly connected to South Australia than ever before. Though he regretted it, Richard Kiliani knew it as well as anyone. In any coming conflict with Germany, he predicted, South Australian Germans would be of no political use to Germany.[36]

The roots, then, of the disaster in Anglo-German relations that was about to unfold with the outbreak of war, must be sought not just in the views or actions of German Australians, or indeed in the international tensions that accompanied the age of imperial rivalry. Rather, it must be remembered that in

Australia, too, the genie of nationalism had been unleashed well before war was declared. Federation had brought Australia its own version of unification: a process of nation-building had been set in motion that, as never before, would prove remarkably intolerant of the presence of the 'other'. While it was already clear that the Australian identity being formed before the outbreak of war was that of a 'White Australia', it was not yet apparent to what extent that identity would be not just white but 'Anglo'. And more than at any earlier point in Australian history, it would be an exclusive identity, as German South Australians were about to discover to their detriment and dismay.

10

Irish South Australians in 1914

Unconditional imperial loyalty?

STEPHANIE JAMES

On Monday 1 June 1914, Adelaide's Irish societies combined to organise a public demonstration at the Exhibition Building on North Terrace.[1] The gathering was carefully engineered to show the extent of South Australia's support for the Home Rule Bill, which a few days earlier had passed the House of Commons in Britain. This, the Bill's third successful passage through Westminster, terminated opposition from the House of Lords, meaning that Ireland was about to receive a form of self-government equivalent to that existing in the dominions. Adelaide's meeting was huge, attracting over 10,000 people at a time when the city's population was only 190,000. And the demonstration made headline news in Adelaide's three daily papers, the *Register*, *Advertiser* and *Daily Herald* – the latter devoted its editorial to the event.[2] 'Contingents from Gawler, Salisbury, Mount Barker [and] Murray Bridge' were named as attending.[3]

This gathering on a winter Monday night can be seen as making a very clear statement about how Irish South Australians perceived themselves, their place in the local community, and their relationship to the Empire. Equally, reactions to Adelaide's

Home Rule event can be interpreted as powerful declarations about how this minority group was seen by other sections of the community.

An examination of the events of mid-1914, just before the intervention of an Empire-threatening war, provides an opportunity to evaluate both sets of South Australian perceptions. This chapter will argue that the trajectory towards 1914 involved different stages, but that throughout the colonial period and the early twentieth century, both the Catholicism of most Irish immigrants and their numbers were divisive issues in South Australia. The first stage meant negotiating early layers of prejudice and hostility, centring largely on Catholic numbers but also emphasising the quantity, and especially the quality, of Irish immigrants, while after 1880 there was generally greater acceptance.

The argument here, however, is that while Irish-South Australian imperial loyalty was unconditional in 1914, the dominant culture's acceptance of Irish Australians at the same time remained conditional. Even before any issues associated with the First World War emerged in 1914, there was evidence that strong residues of early anti-Irish hostility had persisted. In 1914 the numerical representation of those South Australians claiming Irish descent was just under 15 per cent, a lower percentage than most other states. Lacking the critical mass of Victoria and New South Wales, and the additional visibility derived from either public wealth or community prominence, Irish South Australians lived to some extent with the illusion of their integration. In retrospect, the emphasis on Home Rule revealed the depth of anti-Catholic Irish fault lines; under the stress of war, the conditional nature of the acceptance was revealed.

Background of the Home Rule demonstration and details of its resolutions

Adelaide's Home Rule meeting originated within the United Irish League (UIL). The history of the UIL stretched back to 1879 with the local branch of the Irish Land League.[4] The UIL maintained close links to the Irish Parliamentary Party (IPP) propelling the Westminster Bill. The League had promoted a number of fundraising and educational visits by a series of party delegates between 1881 and 1912. The Adelaide demonstration in June 1914 had a deliberate strategic objective. Rather than asking politicians to dispatch cables of support to London, the Irish societies jointly planning the meeting decided to invite men from all parties: 'They would thus be able to force [public men] to declare their views, and show on which side they were'.[5]

The meeting to organise the demonstration was chaired by the Speaker of the South Australian House of Assembly, Irish Australian Larry O'Loughlin, in a hall displaying the Irish and Scottish flags as well as the Union Jack.[6] A rousing letter of endorsement from the ailing local Archbishop O'Reily was read by Father R.W. Spence, who was about to be consecrated as O'Reily's coadjutor.[7] Four resolutions were proposed and seconded by politicians, including federal representatives McMahon Glynn, Gregor McGregor, John Newlands and James Vincent O'Loghlin, and state representatives Crawford Vaughan, Bill Denny, Harry Jackson and Thomas Ryan.[8] The first motion congratulated those responsible for the 'restoration of Ireland's parliament' while the third voiced opposition to the potential exclusion of Ulster from Home Rule. The second resolution was the one that excited most immediate acclaim as well as outrage beyond the gathering. It stated:

> That this meeting of citizens of South Australia is of opinion that, in accordance with the most treasured traditions of British Government and British justice, and for the cementing of the Empire into one harmonious whole, Home Rule should be brought into operation under the provisions of the Parliament Act at as early a date as possible.[9]

The final motion moved that all resolutions be immediately cabled to both British Prime Minister Asquith and IPP leader John Redmond.

Thunderous applause and cheers punctuated the meeting, which ended with singing of both the anti-British 'God Save Ireland' and, significantly, 'God Save the King'.[10] Irish South Australians reflected optimism and confidence at this meeting, in relation to imminent Home Rule, but also more broadly about their place in society.

The Irish in the colony's early decades

The sense of optimism in 1914 represented a significant departure from the experience of most Irish Catholics during South Australia's opening decades. Prominent Protestant Irishmen were among early arrivals – in 1850 George Strickland Kingston boasted that on 11 September 1836 he had been 'the first Irishman who landed in South Australia'.[11] Historians, including Eric Richards, have judged them as bringing 'high-level skill to the new colony'.[12] Such men willingly participated with Catholic Irishmen in groups such as the Sons of Erin and St Patrick's Society between 1840 and 1856.[13] These decades, however, revealed significant community hostility towards Catholic residents. Although Douglas Pike concluded in his landmark 1957 work *Paradise of Dissent* that 'a degree

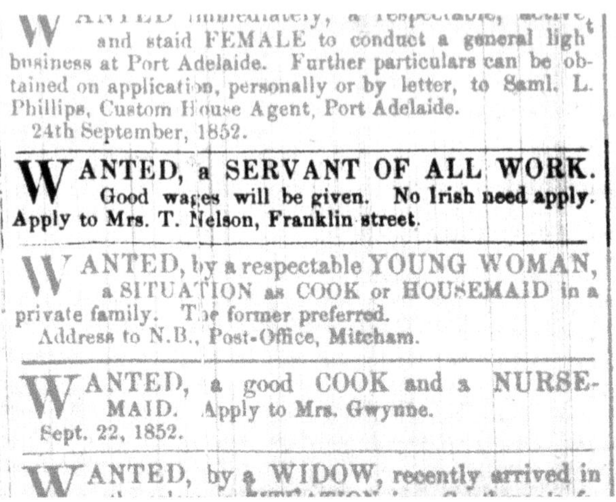

W and staid FEMALE to conduct a general light business at Port Adelaide. Further particulars can be obtained on application, personally or by letter, to Saml. L. Phillips, Custom House Agent, Port Adelaide.
24th September, 1852.

WANTED, a SERVANT OF ALL WORK. Good wages will be given. No Irish need apply. Apply to Mrs. T. Nelson, Franklin street.

WANTED, by a respectable YOUNG WOMAN, a SITUATION as COOK or HOUSEMAID in a private family. The former preferred.
Address to N.B., Post-Office, Mitcham.

WANTED, a good COOK and a NURSE-MAID. Apply to Mrs. Gwynne.
Sept. 22, 1852.

WANTED, by a WIDOW, recently arrived in

Advertisement in South Australian *Register*, 1855.
[*Register*, 24 September 1855]

of anti-Catholicism was … to be expected', he argued that contemporaries and partisan writers exaggerated this.[14]

Margaret Press, author of a two-volume history of Catholicism in South Australia, interprets the situation for Irish immigrants very differently. She insists that 'inherited prejudice … prevailed' more frequently than religious tolerance.[15] Evidence suggests that, while immigrant Irish labour was essential, the Irish themselves were generally unwanted. In 1839 Sydney's senior Catholic cleric, Dr Ullathorne, visited Adelaide when the Catholic population was perhaps fifty, and he encountered opposition from all layers of officialdom. Struggling to get an appointment with the governor, he also failed to gain access to 'a building which had been lent to every denomination until they had a place of worship of their own'.[16] Resistance to Irish immigration was evident in the official response received by the non-sectarian St Patrick's Society to its call for equalisation of migration numbers from the mother country. In 1849, the group's memorial (or petition) to Colonial Secretary Earl Grey 'sought to vindicate the character of the labouring Irish who had settled in this Province'. The Colonial Office response revealed how London viewed local attitudes to the Irish: it doubted whether moves to increase Irish emigration 'would be acceptable to the majority of settlers in [South Australia]'.[17] These early decades reflected two important strands for Irish South Australians, one related to evidence of cooperation and support across religious lines within this community of Irish, while the other pointed to very specific bias against Irish Catholics.

The 1850s witnessed more extreme and negative responses to Irish immigration – including overt statements, editorials, news items and job advertisements – and all these reflected what the *Register*'s editor described in April 1850 as 'the prejudice and antipathy with which the Irish are generally regarded'.[18] In January an article taken from the *Edinburgh Review* and published in the *Register* proclaimed that 'The Irishman improves in two or three years by emigrating to Australia'. Between 1852 and 1880, 15 job advertisements in the *Register* stated that 'No Irish Need Apply'; significantly, 11 of these were before mid-1855.[19] Margaret Press emphasises that large numbers of Irish arrivals in the 1850s were seen as threatening local employment. Moreover, her explanation pinpoints the intersection between religion, ethnicity and culture:

> Although many of these Irish immigrants were not Catholic, opposition to the Irish became for many people synonymous with opposition to Catholicism, and there was expressed a fear

that the basically British colony would become swamped by a different cultural tradition.[20]

These concerns about Irish difference in a British society continued to swirl around South Australia, with the First World War probably representing the highest point of concern. Mismatched immigrant supply and demand – which emerged as an issue in 1855 and 1856 when 1258 young Irishwomen arrived between January and June 1855 – was an inevitable consequence of distance and changing economic circumstances. However, the surplus was intensified by public disturbances at the Female Immigration Depot and further reinforced by the perceived domestic limitations of some female Irish immigrants.[21] The Immigration Agent's Report judged them as 'so thoroughly useless that they are literally not worth their wages'.[22] The solution implemented in 1855 – dispersal through rural servants' depots (including in Clare, Mount Barker and Willunga) – helped dilute community antagonism and widened the pool of marriageable young women in these rural areas.[23] But events of this decade made lasting impressions on public memory.[24]

Varying challenges of the 1860s

Immigration numbers in the 1860s continued to excite controversy about 'Irishness' in South Australia, as becomes clear from even a small number of examples. In 1860, when discussing the previous year's Immigration Agent's Report, the editor of the *Advertiser* noted the imbalance between nominated and selected individuals. Had the former been 'a useful class' instead of those nominated by the 'fatal [Irish] arrivals of 1854 and 1855', and thus 'more ignorant and less suited to the conditions of the labour market', the incoming might have proved worthy immigrants.[25] Then the 1862 appointment of an Irish-Catholic governor, Sir Dominick Daly (not only the first to any Australian colony, but to the colony with fewest Irish and greatest antipathy), met with initial hostility.[26] At a South Australian Benefit Society dinner the following year, the chairman's toast to the governor (in his absence) stated that 'His Excellency arrived under the most unfavourable circumstances, as the idea of a Catholic governor bringing all manner of evils among them was entertained by many'.[27] Historian Peter Howell judged Daly as being 'relatively harmless' and having previously served the Empire well but being 'too far past his prime' when appointed to South Australia: 'He carried out his duties perfunctorily, and died in office in 1868'.[28] However, comment from the City Correspondent of the *Kapunda Herald* about the possibility of '[a]nother Irishman to rule over us' following Daly's death revealed both antipathy and condescension towards the Irish. In referring to Daly and his Protestant Irish predecessor, Sir Richard MacDonnell, the correspondent wrote:

> Why the Colonial Secretary must suppose that South Australia is a second edition of Tipperary ... Sir Richard MacDonnell was great in the smart young man sort of style. Sir Dominick was a pattern of many un-Hibernian qualities – a type of the open-hearted, affable cosmopolitan.[29]

The statement, as well as hinting at the ethnicity and culture divide mentioned above, revealed inherent prejudice about 'Irish' qualities.

The *Register*'s 1862 St Patrick's Day analysis of the local Irish provides a very explicit précis of the more common stereotypes applied to the Irish. While the item does acknowledge change,

Sir Dominick Daly, Irish-born Governor of South Australia from 4 March 1862 to 19 February 1868. He was also Australia's first Irish Governor. [SLSA B 5973]

the strength of its negative judgement of Irish colonists was pervasive. Adelaide was said:

> to have had its characteristic celebrations heretofore, the sons of the sod having dined and fought after dinner as if their poteen was brewed in bogs or fastnesses where law and order were unknown ... [But] Pat in Adelaide seldom breaks the law or a friend's head: he has lost half his fun but has doubled his industry.[30]

This daily paper's subtext seems clear: Irish colonists are acceptable but only on terms demonstrating the discarding of identifiable 'Irish' traits – poverty, violence, drinking and lack of education – and their replacement with more suitable ones.

Qualities such as industriousness and education were

proffered as pathways towards 'manfully better[ing] his condition'.[31] In an environment where the clarity and universality of prejudice and judgement was strong, the Irish were a minority that was both visible in terms of religion and surnames, and audible in terms of the brogue.

Figures in 1862 revealed that 60 per cent of colonial assisted passages between 1836 and 1861 had brought Irish to the colony.[32] This proportion was confronting for those anxious to maintain an Anglo-dominant society. When, in March 1868, Irishman Henry O'Farrell attempted to assassinate the first royal colonial visitor, Prince Alfred, this developed as an extremely anxious time for South Australia's Irish community. Unlike other colonies, where the crime precipitated intense and violent hostility, evidence underlines that the local Irish demonstrated appropriate levels both of imperial devotion and indignation towards the assassin.[33] After the Town Hall sympathy meeting on 16 March, the *Register* noted approvingly that Irishmen uttered 'stronger denunciation[s] of O'Farrell's outrage than any which Anglo-Saxon tongues could compass'.[34] The Catholic newspaper's editorial captured the Irish-Catholic sentiment, describing 'deep dismay' at the news, waiting 'with bated breath to see the result of the public meeting' with fears of 'religious animosity and national prejudices' followed by huge relief. The clerical editor judged that the atmosphere 'was a beautiful proof that in South Australia we are one united nation, untroubled by the thought of the country that gave us birth or our religion'.[35] Whether this conclusion of unconditional acceptance in the late 1860s was soundly based is important in terms of the Irish community's subsequent appreciation of the perceptions of the wider society, something the visible prejudice in 1914 suggests was misunderstood.[36]

Immigrant numbers and lingering prejudices from 1870 to 1900

Immigration continued to arouse public questions in the later 1870s and 1880s. The reintroduction of the nomination system brought another 4000 Irish newcomers to the colony between 1876 and 1880, many from Ulster.[37] In 1878, for example, incoming Irish exceeded others from Britain by 400.[38] Irish nominations for assisted passages grew from the nine per cent figure of the colonial total in 1853 to 47 per cent five years later, and 67 per cent by 1885.[39] Frequently voiced concerns from newspaper correspondents related either to immigrant economic impact or to the possibility of incoming migrants destabilising 'the ethnic and religious demography of the settlement'.[40] And as newspaper coverage of St Patrick's Day in 1879 reveals, a strongly critical, if not prejudiced, subtext remained. In a largely positive description of the day's events (the procession that halted outside Government House for bands to play the national anthem, the sports at the exhibition ground and the concert with its dancing), the nuanced judgement was powerful:

> But the most pleasing observation of the visitor was the excellent order that was manifested everywhere, and the almost complete absence of any exhibition of drunkenness. This is especially noteworthy and redounds to the credit of the Catholic community.[41]

Visitor expectations of disorder and drunkenness from the Catholic Irish were clear.

By the 1890s, such innuendos were absent from coverage of the 'national day,' but there were other concerns. In 1894 St Patrick's Day was acknowledged 'as a special occasion on which to sympathise with Ireland in her sufferings and sorrows' as well as an opportunity to 'rejoice with her in the hopes and aspirations that are now guiding her to the "haven of rest" which Irishmen and their friends believe political freedom to be'.[42] However, two years later, newly appointed Archbishop O'Reily made an autocratic (and, according to *Southern Cross* reports, very unpopular) decision to siphon proceeds of the day towards defraying the huge diocesan debt he had inherited.[43] In response, *Register* editorial comment raised concerns about sectarianism. The editor regretted that the 'purely national character of the Irish holiday ... should not find fuller recognition in the celebrations'. Characterising the Archbishop's decision as 'very controversial', the editorial alluded to consequences of excluding Protestant Irishmen by emphasising that 'it cannot be forgotten that sectarian prejudices are easy to arouse but difficult to allay'.[44]

A day later, following the announcement that James Vincent O'Loghlin would be the Chief Secretary in Charles Cameron Kingston's ministry, the *Register* editorial suggested there was 'no little public apprehension' about the appointment because of other factors, such as his Catholicism.[45] O'Loghlin's identification with Catholic *and* Irish issues represented a threat in some quarters.[46] He was founding editor of the successful Irish-Catholic newspaper, the *Southern Cross* (its masthead proclaiming it 'A Journal of Catholic, Irish and General News'), had a close association with every Irish-Australian organisation from the 1880s, and was a frequent contributor to newspaper discussion of Irish issues. His appointment represented the Irish-Catholic minority's success in public life, a development unwelcomed by those accustomed to viewing Irish Catholics through a negative lens.

O'Loghlin was instrumental in planning every IPP delegation

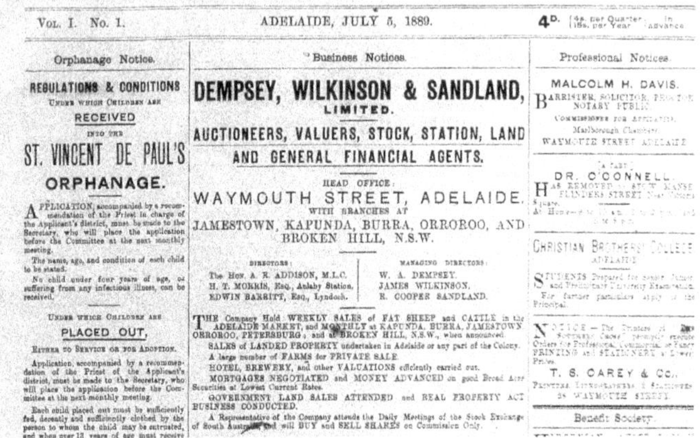

The Southern Cross:

A Weekly Record of Catholic, Irish, and General News.

VOL. I. No. 1. ADELAIDE, JULY 5, 1889. 4D. 4s. per Quarter, 15s. per Year In Advance

Orphanage Notice.

REGULATIONS & CONDITIONS UNDER WHICH CHILDREN ARE RECEIVED INTO THE ST. VINCENT DE PAUL'S ORPHANAGE.

APPLICATION, accompanied by a recommendation of the Priest in charge of the Applicant's district, must be made to the Secretary, who will place the application before the Committee at the next monthly meeting.

The name, age, and condition of each child to be stated.

No child under four years of age, or suffering from any infectious illness, can be received.

UNDER WHICH CHILDREN ARE PLACED OUT, EITHER TO SERVICE OR FOR ADOPTION.

Application, accompanied by a recommendation of the Priest of the Applicant's district, must be made to the Secretary, who will place the application before the Committee at the next monthly meeting.

Each child placed out must be sufficiently fed, decently and sufficiently clothed by the person to whom the child may be entrusted, and when over 12 years of age must receive

Business Notices.

DEMPSEY, WILKINSON & SANDLAND, LIMITED.

AUCTIONEERS, VALUERS, STOCK, STATION, LAND AND GENERAL FINANCIAL AGENTS.

HEAD OFFICE: WAYMOUTH STREET, ADELAIDE. WITH BRANCHES AT JAMESTOWN, KAPUNDA, BURRA, ORROROO, AND BROKEN HILL, N.S.W.

DIRECTORS: The Hon. A. R. ADDISON, M.L.C. H. T. MORRIS, Esq., Anlaby Station. EDWIN BARRITT, Esq., Lyndoch.

MANAGING DIRECTORS: W. A. DEMPSEY. JAMES WILKINSON. R. COOPER SANDLAND.

THE Company Hold WEEKLY SALES of FAT SHEEP and CATTLE in the ADELAIDE MARKET, and MONTHLY at KAPUNDA, BURRA, JAMESTOWN ORROROO, PETERSBURG, and at BROKEN HILL, N.S.W., when announced.

SALES of LANDED PROPERTY undertaken in Adelaide or any part of the Colony.

A large number of FARMS for PRIVATE SALE.

HOTEL, BREWERY, and other VALUATIONS efficiently carried out.

MORTGAGES NEGOTIATED and MONEY ADVANCED on good Broad Acre Securities at Lowest Current Rates.

GOVERNMENT LAND SALES ATTENDED and REAL PROPERTY ACT BUSINESS CONDUCTED.

A Representative of the Company attends the Daily Meetings of the Stock Exchange of South Australia, and will BUY and SELL SHARES on Commission Only.

Professional Notices.

MALCOLM H. DAVIS. BARRISTER, SOLICITOR, NOTARY PUBLIC. Marlborough Chambers WAYMOUTH STREET ADELAIDE

DR. O'CONNELL

CHRISTIAN BROTHERS' COLLEGE ADELAIDE

T. S. CAREY & Co.

Benefit Society.

Masthead from first issue of Adelaide's *Southern Cross*, 5 July 1889.
[Courtesy of *The Southern Cross*, Adelaide]

visit to South Australia from 1881. These visits between 1881 and 1912 (see Table 1) presented important opportunities for community measurement of Irish-South Australian loyalty. Given that the agenda motivating these visiting Irishmen was essentially critical of imperial government policy towards Ireland, and that delegate meetings across the colony attracted large numbers and raised substantial sums, loyalist community responses might have been extreme. However, as recent research by local historian Fidelma Breen demonstrates convincingly, this was not the case. There were lone voices of anti-Irish prejudice crying in the wilderness of general support for Ireland receiving the same democratic rights as existed in South Australia. Breen charts the growing official recognition of the delegations, from the original silence in 1881, a largely Catholic-only welcome to the Redmond brothers in 1883, greater support for John Dillon in 1889, much more so for the famed Michael Davitt in 1895, and by 1911, a lunch at Government House for the last delegates.[47]

Table 1. IPP Visits: Delegates, dates and amounts raised[48]

Year/s	Delegate/s	Dates	Amounts raised
1881	John W. Walshe	June arrival	£6,130 by early 1883
1883	John & William Redmond	February–November	£15,000–£40,000
1889	John Dillon, John Deasy & Sir Thos Esmonde	March–September	£35,000–£40,000
1906	Joseph Devlin & John T. Donovan	April–August	£22,000
1911–1912	Wm A.K. Redmond, John T. Donovan & Richard Hazelton	October 1911–May 1912	£30,000

Breen's work is consistent with earlier findings by Jenny Stock about the 'very nature of Irishness' differing in South Australia in comparison to the larger colonies (later states), showing that 'Home Rulers were moderate, conservative figures well connected in society though not generally wealthy'.[49] Further, Breen claims that the size of the colonial South Australian Irish community, far from being a disadvantage, 'concentrated the potency of their cultural capital and ... facilitated the success of the Home Rule movement in a Protestant and British colony'.[50] Geography enabled links between Irish community leaders and their non-Irish counterparts in business, politics and sport. This,

Breen suggests, gave 'ordinary Irishmen ... [the] opportunity to simultaneously partake in a respectable local [Home Rule] event patronised by many of the colony's dignitaries and parliamentarians[,] *and* support his fellow countrymen in Ireland'.[51] Thus what could have become tipping points for wider community criticism – the repeated visits of prominent Irish figures who opposed British policies in Ireland – seemed to follow an increasingly unchallenged path of community acceptance.

Snapshots of early twentieth-century sentiment: Irish-Australian and secular press

The years preceding the Great War provide contradictory evidence about local Irish understanding of community attitudes. For example, after the first toast to the king at the 1905 St Patrick's Day dinner – where O'Loghlin presided – the overtly loyal gathering sang the first verse of 'God Save the King'. The *Southern Cross* editor enthused that 'It was evident that the Irishmen present recognised that at long last they had a friend in the Sovereign', an acknowledgement of differences in attitude between King Edward and Queen Victoria.[52] However, features of 1906 (to be further discussed below), after the Federal Parliament passed resolutions in favour of Home Rule in October 1905, revealed substantial community antagonism.

On the other hand, there is surprising evidence that Irish immigration was no longer perceived as the threatening spectre it had been for many decades. In early 1914, after the publication of the 1913 Dominions Royal Commission report, one of South Australia's weekly newspapers with a wide circulation, the *Chronicle*, commented on its immigration focus.[53] The editor, in endorsing the report's recommendations, claimed that:

> There will be general agreement that the Commonwealth would be all the better for the diversion to its shores of a larger share of that stream of emigration from Ireland, a great volume of which now flows to Canada, and in still greater measure to the United States. There are no better colonisers than the Irish, and there are none who take more readily to Agricultural life.[54]

The publication in 1914 of such strong sentiments and their apparently unqualified endorsement of Irish immigrants, in a newspaper with statewide circulation, suggests that public opinion had shifted greatly since the mid-nineteenth century.

Political issues associated with the Home Rule demonstration

Following the 'unprecedented success' of June 1914's 10,000-strong Home Rule meeting, the *Southern Cross* editorial took an understandably congratulatory stand. Adelaide's smaller population and 'the shorter time of preparation' than Melbourne's meeting (which attracted between 40,000 and 45,000) were both heavily emphasised. But the main thrust here, and in the *Daily Herald* and the other dailies, involved those members of both political parties who had neither responded to the invitation nor disclosed their opinion about Home Rule. Leading a Liberal Union government, Premier Peake came in for particular criticism given his refusal to propose a resolution or participate in a meeting that he described as 'outside the scope of Australian legislation'. The *Southern Cross* editor regretted the 'rank and file of the Liberal Party ... generally followed the policy of abstention and neutrality set by Mr Peake and Ministers'. Most of the twenty parliamentarians who attended Adelaide's demonstration, like those in Melbourne, were Labor men. MHR and Irishman Patrick McMahon Glynn, a Liberal, refuted Peake's justification at the Exhibition Hall gathering. The *Southern Cross* also contrasted Peake's evasion with his 1913 statement when he was being dined by the IPP leadership in Dublin. Then proclaiming himself a Home Ruler, Peake had argued the measure 'would help to blend together all parts of the British Empire'.[55]

Table 2 highlights interesting characteristics about those politicians who were willing to attend, in particular their backgrounds and religious affiliation. Together, these suggest an overall societal acceptance of the Irish-Catholic minority. At the same time, the preponderance of Labor men indicates some conservative unwillingness to be publicly identified either with a position embodying criticism of British policy, or a stance almost certainly attracting opposition from community ultra-loyalists; only four Liberal Union supporters were present.[56] Interestingly, only five speakers were Catholic, while six were of Irish heritage or birth. Half the speakers were locally born while others were mostly of Scottish or English birth, but included a solitary German. The religious background of seven speakers was unknown or non-existent.[57] Most of the remaining eight were Anglican, with equal numbers of Congregationalists and Methodists and one Presbyterian, perhaps an early twentieth-century reflection of the state's non-conformist beginnings. Nine men represented the young Commonwealth: four Senators and five Members of the House of Representatives. Labor's over-representation at this meeting probably mirrored major voting trends within the Irish-Catholic population.[58]

Table 2. Parliamentarians at Adelaide 1914 Home Rule Meeting[59]

Name	Position	Religion	Birthplace	Party
W.O. Archibald	MHR*	n/a	England	Labor
F.W. Coneybeer	MHA	Anglican	England	Labor
G. Dankel	MHR*	n/a	Germany	Labor
W.J. Denny	MHA	Catholic	SA**	Labor
P.M. Glynn	MHR*	Catholic	Ireland	Liberal
H. Jackson	MHA	n/a	England	Labor
E.L.M. Klauer	MLC	Anglican	SA	Labor
G. McGregor	Senate*	Presbyterian	Scotland	Labor
W. Miller	MHA	n/a	Scotland	Liberal
J. Newlands	Senate*	Congregational	Scotland	Labor
J.V. O'Loghlin	Senate*	Catholic	SA**	Labor
L. O'Loughlin	MHA	Catholic	SA**	Labor
A. Poynton	MHR*	n/a	SA	Labor
T. Ryan	MHA	n/a	Ireland	Labor
W. Senior	Senate*	Methodist	England	Labor
J.W. Shannon	Senate*	Congregational	SA	Liberal
J.A. Southwood	MHA	Methodist	SA	Labor
J. Travers	MHA	Catholic	SA**	Liberal
C. Vaughan	MHA	Anglican	SA	Labor
G.E. Yates	MHR*	n/a	SA	Labor

* Denotes members of Australia's Commonwealth Parliament.
** Indicates those of Irish background.

Opposition to Home Rule in South Australia

The *Southern Cross* editorial of 3 July had noted that anti-Home Rulers were 'taking notes' at the Exhibition Hall meeting. Letters to the editor during June and July reflected a high volume of negative sentiment. An examination of Adelaide's three daily morning papers reveals at least 18 pro-Home Rule letters and 13 in strong opposition. Another nine claimed to hold non-partisan positions. It is possible that these hostile correspondents only represented a remote response to the intense anxiety generated in Ulster over imminent Home Rule and fears of Rome Rule; nevertheless, they revealed the survival of strident anti-Catholic-Irish feeling. Evidence of such local hostility just prior to the war suggests those decades of acceptance were distinctly conditional. Breen points to the delayed and 'not welcomed' local appearance of Orange Lodges (fraternal organisations committed to defending Protestant civil and religious liberties, of which there were only seven in 1877).[60] While her evidence shows little Lodge interest in Home Rule, membership growth from 379 to 2000 between 1899 and 1903 indicates the emergence of a network capable of generating hostility.[61] It may have been muted, but April 1906's anti-Home Rule meeting at the Town Hall reflected some community ill feeling towards Irish-Catholic aspirations. The gathering followed federal support for Home Rule in 1905 – a Senate vote of 25 to 5 and in the House of Representatives a majority of 33 to 21.[62] The *Southern Cross* noted that opposition had 'spread' to Adelaide, naming the central committee and charging that the 'slimy trail of the Orange Society can be seen through the whole business'.[63] From South Australia came 20,000 signatures to form part of the anti-Home Rule petition of 75,832 presented to the Governor-General in July.[64] Although the parliamentary vote might have reinforced Irish-Catholic South Australians' peace of mind about Ireland's future, Protestant loyalists insisted that such a vote was not representative of the true wishes of Australian citizens.[65] Flexing their loyalist muscle, this group communicated their opposition to London.

In June and July 1914 – following the powerful demonstration of support at the Exhibition Building – the anti-Home Rule lobby, the Ulster Defence League, defiantly organised counter gatherings. Their resolutions disputed that the pro-Home Rule meeting had 'express[ed] the opinion of the majority of our fellow-citizens'.[66] Relatively small suburban meetings followed – 500 at a Norwood gathering, and an unknown number at Hindmarsh – but on 16 July the Exhibition Building attracted a crowd of 3000 to hear an Irish academic from Sydney.[67] Reverend Digges La Touche, supported by a cross-section of Protestant clergymen, painted alarming pictures of Irish-Catholic disloyalty witnessed by him in Dublin.[68] Further meetings were staged at both Kadina and Burra.[69] And in late July the Ulster Defence League of South Australia cabled the proceeds of their collection at the demonstration, a 'first instalment' of £300 for the Ulster Fund.[70]

Just before the war, evidence of strong local opposition to Home Rule was clear, and thus any community support for such Empire-destabilising measures was likely to be interpreted negatively. But South Australia's Irish-Catholics, jubilant about the proximity of Home Rule, seemed unable to recognise the depth, and arguably the extent, of anti-Catholic and anti-Irish feeling in their environment. These sentiments were to be intensified when the Empire was under threat, as it was within weeks of these events.

Conclusion

The outbreak of the First World War coincided with most Irish South Australians enjoying unprecedented confidence about Ireland's future, and apparently feeling secure about their place in society. This community's total support for the war in August

1914 can be clearly tracked through pages of the *Southern Cross*. Imperial loyalty was unqualified, and gratitude for British intervention to save poor little Catholic Belgium was unstinting. But public statements in early October 1914 show that Catholic loyalty was open to question:

> It seems strange to have it dinned into our ears that Catholics cannot be loyal subjects and good citizens, and that their allegiance is divided between the church and the land they lived in ... When the call came in Australia to come forward and fight for the Empire it was responded to, and promptly by members of the Christian Brothers Old Collegians Association.[71]

Claims of Catholic disloyalty thus emerged quickly, but in retrospect, given the nature of opposition to Irish Home Rule just before the war and the negative colonial legacy, which incorporated both immigration issues and Catholicism, these wartime accusations are unsurprising. From 1916 Dublin's Easter Rising and Australia's conscription plebiscites made it clear that, like German South Australians but for different reasons, the acceptance of Irish South Australians had only ever been conditional. The deep-seated prejudice emerging from 1916 indicates these sentiments had been dormant rather than extinct, as had been generally perceived by the Irish. Irish colonial transgressions threatened the new society's Britishness, but post-Federation, powerful groups identified Irish-Australian support for Home Rule with the disintegration of Empire. Largely unconditional Irish-Australian imperial loyalty in 1914 was insufficient to neutralise, much less delete, their non-Anglo-Saxon background.

Notes

Chapter 1 ~ Progressive conservatism and boundless optimism

1 Reserve Bank of Australia (RBA), 'Catherine Helen Spence (1825–1910)', *Banknotes*, accessed 7 July 2016, http://banknotes.rba.gov.au/australias-banknotes/people-on-the-banknotes/catherine-helen-spence; Susan Magarey, 'Catherine Helen Spence', *Adelaidia*, accessed 7 July 2016, http://adelaidia.sa.gov.au/people/catherine-helen-spence.

2 RBA, 'Catherine Helen Spence'; Susan Eade, 'Spence, Catherine Helen (1825–1910)', Australian Dictionary of Biography (ADB), National Centre of Biography (NCB), Australian National University (ANU), published first in hardcopy 1976, accessed 20 June 2016, http://addb.anu.edu.au/biography/spence-catherine-helen-4627/text7621.

3 P.A. Howell, *South Australia and Federation* (Adelaide: Wakefield Press, 2002), 256.

4 Philip Jones, 'Unaipon, David (1872–1967), ADB, NCB, ANU, published first in hardcopy 1990, accessed 13 May 2016, http://adb.anu.edu.au/biography/unaipon-david-8898/text15631; South Australian Parliamentary Papers (SAPP), *Progress Report of the Royal Commission on the Aborigines*, no. 26 (Adelaide: Government Printer, 1913), 618.

5 Australian Antarctic Division, 'Sir Douglas Mawson (1882–1958)', accessed 14 June 2016, http://www.antarctica.gov.au/about-antarctica/history/people/douglas-mawson.

6 Australian Antarctic Division, 'Sir Douglas Mawson'; F.J. Jacka, 'Mawson, Sir Douglas (1882–1958)', ADB, NCB, ANU, published first in hardcopy 1986, accessed 13 May 2016, http://adb.anu.edu.au/biography/mawson-sir-douglas-7531/text12563.

7 T.L. Stevenson, 'Population Change Since 1836', in *The Flinders History of South Australia, Social History (FHSA, SA)*, ed. Eric Richards (Adelaide: Wakefield Press, 1986), 177; Michael Williams, *The Changing Rural Landscape of South Australia*, 2nd Edition (Adelaide: State Publishing, South Australia, 1992),17–18.

8 Official Year Book of the Commonwealth of Australia, 1901–1913, no. 7, 1914, 10.

9 Stevenson, 'Population Change Since 1836'; Robert Foster and Tom Gara, 'Aboriginal Culture in South Australia'; see also, John Summers, 'Colonial Race Relations'; all in *FHSA, SA*,175, 65, 283–284.

10 Official Year Book of the Commonwealth of Australia, 1901–1913, 10.

11 I. A. Harmstorf, 'Germans', in *The Wakefield Companion to South Australian History*, ed. Wilfrid Prest, Kerrie Round and Carol Fort (Adelaide: Wakefield Press, 2001), 224–225.

12 Howell, *South Australia and Federation*, 61.

13 Howell, *South Australia and Federation*, 218–219.

14 Howell, *South Australia and Federation*, 214–215.

15 P.A. Howell, *South Australia and Federation*, 213.

16 Joan Hancock and Eric Richards, 'Wealth, Work and Well Being: Some Historical Indicators', in *FHSA, SA*, 596.

17 'Harvester Judgement', *Defining Moments in Australian History,* National Museum of Australia, accessed 21 July 2016, http://www.nma.gov.au/online_features/defining_moments/featured/harvester_judgement.

18 Although Victoria and Queensland had introduced state age pension schemes and New South Wales, age and invalid schemes, South Australia had not done so.

19 Statutory regulations denied age and invalid pensions to indigenes of Australia, the Pacific Islands, New Zealand and Africa. P.A. Howell, *South Australia and Federation*, 355.

20 Hancock and Richards, 'Wealth, Work and Well Being', 596.

21 W.A. Sinclair, 'Women at Work in Melbourne and Adelaide Since 1871', *Economic Record* 57 (1981): 344–353; W.A. Sinclair, 'Women and Economic Change in Melbourne 1871–1921', *Historical Studies* 20 (1982–1983): 288–290.

22 SAPP, *Population and Vital, Table No. 17, Occupations-Census 1911 and 1921*, no. 1 (Adelaide: Government Printer, 1924).

23 Tom Sheridan, 'Strikes', in *The Wakefield Companion to South Australian History*, 519–520; P.A. Howell, *South Australia and Federation*, 314; Philip Payton, *One and All; Labor and the Radical Tradition in South Australia* (Adelaide: Wakefield Press, 2016), 177–182.

24 Hancock and Richards, 'Wealth, Work and Well Being', 598.

25 See, for example, the essay by Susan Magarey, 'Catherine Helen Spence's Journalism: *Some Social Aspects of South Australian Life,* by A Colonist of 1839 – C.H. Spence', *Journal of the Historical Society of South Australia (JHSSA)* 41 (2013): 22–29.

26 Margrette Kleinig, '"Mrs. Moore is most energetic and devoted to her work": Bessie Moore 1859–1923, a career public servant', *JHSSA* 42 (2014): 82 and 89.

27 *South Australian Acts*, 'Female Law Practitioners Act', no. 1050, 1911.

28 Jack Cross, *Great Central State, The Foundation of the Northern Territory* (Adelaide: Wakefield Press, 2011), 370–371.

29 Payton, *One and All*, 182–185.

30 Gordon D. Combe, MC, *Responsible Government in South Australia, Volume One*, revised edition (Adelaide: Wakefield Press, 2009), 146.
31 Combe, *Responsible Government in South Australia*, 146.
32 Hancock and Richards, 'Wealth, Work and Well Being, 587.
33 Combe, *Responsible Government in South Australia*, 143.
34 Howell, *South Australia and Federation*, 293.
35 Howell, *South Australia and Federation*, 315–317.
36 Cross, *Great Central State*, 370–371.
37 Combe, *Responsible Government in South Australia*, 148; Howell, *South Australia and Federation*, 329. The agreement was also applicable to the lower waters of the Murrumbidgee and Darling Rivers.
38 Howell gives a summary of this interesting legal matter in *South Australia and Federation*, 368–372.
39 Ian B. Bates, 'G.H. Michell & Sons (Aust) Pty Ltd'; Angela Heuzenroeder, 'B. Seppelt & Sons'; 'Reynell Family'; in *The Wakefield Companion to South Australian History*, 349, 484–485, 458–459; Joan Hancock and Eric Richards, 'Holden, Henry James (1859–1926)', ADB, NCG, ANU, published first in hardcopy 1983, accessed 7 October 2016, http://addb.anu.edu.au/biography/holden-henry-james-6704/text11571.
40 'Alfred Simpson' in *The Wakefield Companion to South Australian History*, 490–491; State Library of SA, 'World War One', *Australian Red Cross: South Australian Division*, accessed 8 January 2016, http://guides.slsa.sa.gov.au/c.php?g=410369&p=2795695; 'Death of Mr. A.A. Simpson', *Advertiser*, 28 November 1939, 12.
41 Department of Immigration & Ethnic Affairs, *Australian Immigration Consolidated Statistics*, no. 13, (Canberra: Government Printer, 1983), Table 4.
42 Encapsulated in the introduction to the second reading of the 'Immigration Bill', *South Australian Parliamentary Debates* (SAPD), July–December 1911, 111; 'Assisted Immigration', *Register*, 3 March 1911.
43 SAPP, *Immigration Acts, 1911 and 1913 – Additional Regulations*, no. 30 (Adelaide: Government Printer, 1914), 3.
44 South Australia and New South Wales were the only Australian states in which the birthrate rose in this period. Margrette Kleinig, '"She keeps the silver in excellent order", Government-Assisted Emigration of Female Domestic Servants from The United Kingdom to South Australia, 1873–1939' (PhD thesis, Flinders University, 2007), 26.
45 *Advertiser*, 5 August 1914, 13.

Chapter 2 ~ South Australia from the Boer War to the Great War

1 This article is based on a paper delivered by Dr J.C. Bannon to the symposium *South Australia on the Eve of War* at the University of Adelaide on 2 August 2014. It also draws on an article by the author, 'Great Federal Expectations: South Australia and the Commonwealth', in *The Politics of Democracy in South Australia: a compilation of papers* (Adelaide: Electoral Commission of South Australia and the History Trust of South Australia, 2007), 65–72.

2 J.C. Bannon, 'South Australia', in *The Centenary Companion to Australian Federation*, ed. Helen Irving (Melbourne: Cambridge University Press, 1999), 129–186, particularly pages 165–168; P.A. Howell, 'The Strongest Delegation: The South Australians at the Constitutional Convention of 1897–8,' *The New Federalist* 1 (1998): 44–50; R.L. Reid, 'South Australian Politicians and the Proposals for Federation', in *Melbourne Studies in Education 1960–61*, ed. E.L. French, (Melbourne: Melbourne University Press, 1962), 204–219.

3 T. Price, Premier, *Memorandum for His Excellency the Governor as to the proposed Colonial Conference of 1907*, Chief Secretary's Office, GRG/24/90/450, State Records of South Australia (SRSA), Adelaide.

4 In Western Australia, women had voted in 1900 in the last minute-decision of that colony to join.

5 See J.C. Bannon, *Supreme Federalist: The Political Life of Sir John Downer* (Adelaide: Wakefield Press, 2009), 191–195.

6 All this is well-described by Jack Cross in *Great Central State: The Foundation of the Northern Territory* (Adelaide: Wakefield Press, 2011).

7 J. Quick, and R.R. Garran, *The Annotated Constitution of the Australian Commonwealth* (Sydney: Angus & Robertson, 1901), 612–613.

8 Stephanie McCarthy, *Tom Price: from Stonecutter to Premier* (Adelaide: Wakefield Press, 2015), 183.

9 For this and subsequent election information see Dean Jaensch, *History of South Australian Elections 1856–2006, Volume 1 House of Assembly, Volume 2 Legislative Council* (Adelaide: History Trust of South Australia & State Electoral Office of South Australia, 2007). For ministerial and parliamentary information see Clerk of the Parliaments & Clerk of the Legislative Council (Compilers), *Statistical Record of the Legislature, 1836–2007* (Adelaide: Parliament of South Australia, 2007).

10 The first was a ministry formed by Anderson Dawson in Queensland in 1899, which lasted only a week; Price's lasted nearly four years.

11 The chief source of the figures in this and following passages are Wray Vamplew, ed., *Australians: Historical Statistics* (Sydney: Fairfax, Syme and Weldon Associates, 1987), and Trevor Griffin and Murray McCaskill, eds, *Atlas of South Australia* (Adelaide: South Australian Government Printer & Wakefield Press, 1986).

12 For the following passages see Craig Wilcox, *Australia's Boer War: The War in South Africa 1899–1902* (Melbourne: Oxford University Press, 2002), and J.C. Bannon, 'A War for a Constitution: The Australian Colonies and the South African War', *The New Federalist* 5, (2000): 2–10.

Chapter 3 ~ New women and the modern family

1 Their return to the city was reported in the *Southern Argus* on 20 January 1910, 2. Gertrude and James Anderson were Margaret Anderson's paternal grandparents.

2 Reported in the *Register*, 15 December 1900, 3, and the *Chronicle*, 21 December 1901, 33.

3 The engagement was reported in the *Chronicle*, 9 June 1906, 51.

4 For example at the Lyric theatre in June 1908, and again in 1909. See *Register*, 17 June 1908, 7, and 4 August 1909, 5.

5 See *Advertiser*, 5 October 1907, 10; *Advertiser* 8 October 1909, 8.

6 See *Herald*, 8 November 1912, 5; *Southern Argus*, 2 January 1913, 3.

7 M. Anderson, 'No sex please we're demographers: nineteenth century fertility decline re-visited', in *Citizenship, Women and Social Justice*, eds. Joy Damousi and Katherine Ellinghouse (Melbourne: University of Melbourne Press, 1999), 251–262. Alison Mackinnon, *Love and Freedom: Professional Women and the Reshaping of Personal Life* (Cambridge: Cambridge University Press, 1997).

8 Mackinnon, *Love and Freedom*, 95–104; Margaret Anderson and Alison Mackinnon, 'Women's agency in the first fertility transition: a debate re-visited', *The History of the Family* 20, no. 1 (2015): 9–23.

9 Even the most isolated and conservative groups, like the rural German Lutherans living in the Adelaide Hills, had smaller families by the 1890s. Margaret Anderson, 'German Women and Fertility in 19th Century South Australia', *Researching German Women Pioneers: Putting the jig-saw together*, proceedings of a workshop held at the University of Adelaide on the 22 May 2010, 35.

10 Mackinnon, *Love and Freedom*, 92–94.

11 Condoms were regarded with distaste by some who associated them with prostitution. They were also expensive.

12 Patricia Sumerling, 'Madam Harpur: the trials and tribulations of an Adelaide doctoress', unpublished paper, 10.

13 Anderson and Mackinnon, 'Women's agency in the first fertility transition', 20–22.

14 *Mail*, 15 March 1913, 9.

15 South Australian Parliamentary Papers (SAPP), *Proceedings*, no. 19 (Adelaide: Government Printer, 1904).

16 *Critic*, 16 September 1899, 18.

17 Mackinnon, *Love and Freedom*, 23 and 103. Gigi Santow, 'Coitus interruptus in the twentieth century', *Population and Development Review*, 19, no. 4 (December 1993): 768.

18 Mackinnon, *Love and Freedom*, 39.

19 Janet McCalman, *Sex and Suffering: Women's Health and a Women's Hospital* (Melbourne: Melbourne University Press, 1998), 127–129 and 154–155.

20 Sumerling, 'Madam Harpur', 10.

21 Reported in the *Register*, 4 April 1913, 10.

22 The long account of the case of Alma Kure cited the evidence of her friend Mrs Creeper, who reputedly tried to persuade Alma to have her baby in one of the 'homes' in Adelaide. *Register*, 4 April 1913, 10.

23 See *Advertiser*, 24 May 1902, 6, or *Chronicle*, 31 May 1902, 34.

24 See *Register*, 8 May 1902, 4.

25 Reported in *Advertiser*, 14 August 1900, 5. See also *Chronicle*, 18 August 1900, 36.

26 Susan Magarey, ed., *Ever yours, C.H. Spence* (Adelaide: Wakefield Press, 2005), 169–170.

27 Helen Jones, *In Her Own Name: Women in South Australian History* (Adelaide: Wakefield Press, 1986), 143.

28 Jones, *In Her Own Name*, 45.

29 Jones, *In Her Own Name*, 64–65. The father's authority ceased on a child reaching majority at the age of 21 years. Equal custody rights were not enacted until 1940.

30 *Advertiser*, 1 February 1912, 8.

31 See *Port Pirie Recorder and North Western Mail*, 8 October 1908, 3.

32 Ann Delroy, 'Domestic gas cooking appliances in metropolitan Perth, 1900–1950', *Records of the Western Australian Museum* 14, no. 4 (1990): 471–472. Metters may have been manufacturing gas stoves in Adelaide by 1913, but no advertisements were found for these stoves in the local newspapers.

33 Cited in Jones, *In Her Own Name*, 184.

34 See *Express and Telegraph*, 17 August 1912, 5.

35 *Register*, 12 January 1911, 4.

36 Her column, entitled 'The Mirror of Fashion', appeared every Saturday.

37 See 'Miss Watkins's Wedding and Bridesmaid's Toilettes', *Mail*, 30 August 1913, 2.

38 All advertised on the front page of the *Mail*, 30 August 1913.

39 In 1911, 14 per cent of women aged 45–49 had never married. Carol Bacchi, 'The "Woman Question" in South Australia', in *The Flinders History of South Australia: Social History*, ed. Eric Richards (Adelaide: Wakefield Press, 1986), 428.

40 In, for example, the *Express and Telegraph*, 6 December 1912, 6.

41 *Daily Herald*, 18 July 1910, 2.

42 *Daily Herald*, 20 March 1912, 4.

43 Jones, *In Her Own Name*, 211.

44 Jones, *In Her Own Name*, 193.

45 *Daily Herald*, 4 April 1911, 4 and 29 September 1910, 2.

46 Reported in *Port Pirie Recorder and North Western Mail*, 1 November 1911, 4.

47 *Daily Herald*, 4 April 1911, 4.

48 *Daily Herald*, 9 March 1914, 3.

Chapter 4 ~ Aboriginal people and the state in South Australia, 1901-1914

1 Please note that this article includes language which is drawn from historical sources and is today considered offensive. It is not my intention to cause offence, but to retain the language as historical evidence of past attitudes (this includes contemporary capitalisation, or lack thereof). Please also note that I am using 'Aboriginal' to refer to Indigenous people in South Australia, following preferred current usage as expressed by that community.

2 For a comprehensive history of the administration of Aboriginal people in South Australia, see Cameron Raynes, *'A Little Flour and a Few Blankets': An Administrative History of Aboriginal Affairs in South Australia, 1834–2000* (Adelaide: State Records of South Australia, 2002).

3 For an overview of the impact of colonisation, see Christobel Mattingley and Ken Hampton, *Survival in Our Own Land: 'Aboriginal' experiences in 'South Australia' since 1836* (Adelaide: Wakefield Press, 1988).

4 For Point McLeay, see Mattingley and Hampton, *Survival in Our Own Land*, 183, and *Report of the Protector of Aborigines, 1901*, 4; for Point Pierce, Mattingley and Hampton, *Survival in Our Own Land*, 197, and *Report of the Protector of Aborigines, 1901*, 4; for Killalpaninna, *Report of the Protector of Aborigines, 1901*, 4; for Koonibba, Mattingley and Hampton, *Survival in Our Own Land*, 203; for Manunka, Raynes, *'A Little Flour and a Few Blankets'*, 30; and for Poonindie, see Peggy Brock and Doreen Kartinyeri, *Poonindie: The Rise and Destruction of an Aboriginal Agricultural Community* (Adelaide: Aboriginal Heritage Branch, 1989), 74.

5 Peggy Brock, 'South Australia', in *Contested Ground: Australian Aborigines under the British Crown*, ed. Ann McGrath (Sydney: Allen & Unwin, 1995), 223.

6 Raynes, *'A Little Flour and a Few Blankets'*, 158; *Report of the Protector of Aborigines, 1901*, 1. This figure can only be regarded as indicative.

7 For a discussion of Aboriginal reserves, see Robert Foster, 'An Imaginary Dominion: The Representation and Treatment of Aborigines in South Australia, 1834–1911' (PhD thesis, University of Adelaide, 1993), and, in brief, Mandy Paul and Robert Foster, 'Married to the Land: Land Grants to Aboriginal Women in South Australia 1848–1911', *Australian Historical Studies* 34, no. 121 (2003).

8 *Report of the Protector of Aborigines, 1901*, 5.

9 Tony Austin, *Simply the Survival of the Fittest: Aboriginal Administration in South Australia's Northern Territory 1863–1910* (Darwin: Historical Society of the Northern Territory, 1992), 88–91.

10 Austin, *Simply the Survival of the Fittest*, 89–91.

11 'The Aborigines Bill', *Adelaide Observer*, 18 November 1899. Thanks to Jude Elton for drawing this petition to my attention.

12 Pat Stretton and Christine Finnimore, 'Black Fellow Citizens: Aborigines and the Commonwealth Franchise', *Australian Historical Studies* 25, no. 101 (1993): 521–535.

13 Foster, *An Imaginary Dominion*, 336.

14 See Paul and Foster, 'Married to the Land'.
15 *Report of the Protector of Aborigines, 1905*, 3.
16 *Report of the Protector of Aborigines, 1907*, 3.
17 Raynes, 'A Little Flour and a Few Blankets', 33; Norm Lalor, 'South, William Garnet (1855–1923)', ADB, ACB, ANU, published first in hardcopy 2005, accessed 21 July 2014, http://adb.anu.edu.au/biography/south-william-garnet-13202.
18 *Report of the Protector of Aborigines, 1908*, 1.
19 *Report of the Protector of Aborigines, 1908*, 1.
20 *Report of the Protector of Aborigines, 1908*, 1.
21 Raynes, *'A Little Flour and a Few Blankets'*, 34.
22 Mattingley and Hampton, *Survival in Our Own Land*, 159. The list is: GRG 52/1/1910/2, SRSA Adelaide.
23 GRG 52/1/1910/22, SRSA, Adelaide, quoted in Mattingley and Hampton, *Survival in Our Own Land*, 159.
24 Austin, *Aboriginal Administration in South Australia's Northern Territory*, 93; and see *The Northern Territory Aboriginals Act*, 1910. This Act shared its subtitle with the South Australian Act: 'An Act to make Provision for the better Protection and Control of the Aboriginal Inhabitants of the Northern Territory and for other purposes'.
25 *South Australian Parliamentary Debates (SAPD), House of Assembly*, 28 September 1910, 617.
26 *SAPD, Legislative Council*, 19 September 1911, 230.
27 *SAPD, Legislative Council*, 19 September 1911, 231.
28 *SAPD, Legislative Council*, 19 September 1911, 231.
29 *SAPD, Legislative Council*, 28 September 1911, 287; see also 325 and 421.
30 See *SAPD, Legislative Council*, 1 November 1911, 420.
31 *SAPD, Legislative Council*, 5 October 1911, 326; see *SAPD, House of Assembly*, 5 September 1911, 417.
32 *SAPD, Legislative Council*, 5 October 1911, 327.
33 *SAPD, House of Assembly*, 5 September 1911, 416–417.
34 *SAPD, Legislative Council*, 17 October 1911, 345. This change was proposed by The Hon. J.J. Duncan: 'possibly it would be as well for the Protector in some cases to retain control after the age of 18'; it was passed without debate.
35 *SAPD, Legislative Council*, 1 November 1911, 421.
36 *SAPD, Legislative Council*, 26 September 1911, 266; see also 325.
37 *SAPD, House of Assembly*, 5 September 1911, 417.
38 *SAPD, Legislative Council*, 17 October 1911, 346.
39 *SAPD, Legislative Council*, 5 October 1911, 327.
40 *Daily Herald*, 29 March 1912, 4.
41 *Report of the Protector of Aborigines, 1912*, 1. See also *Daily Herald*, 29 March 1912, 4.
42 *Report of the Protector of Aborigines*, 1912, 1, 6–7.
43 *Report of the Protector of Aborigines*, 1912, 7.

44 *Daily Herald,* 7 November 1912, 6.
45 *Advertiser,* 14 November 1912, 11.
46 South Australian Parliamentary Papers (SAPP), *Progress Report of the Royal Commission on the Aborigines*, no. 26 (Adelaide: Government Printer, 1913).
47 SAPP, 26 of 1913, vi.
48 SAPP, 26 of 1913, vii.
49 SAPP, *Progress Report of the Royal Commission on the Aborigines*, 113.
50 SAPP, *Progress Report of the Royal Commission on the Aborigines*, 119.
51 SAPP, *Progress Report of the Royal Commission on the Aborigines*, 37.
52 SAPP, *Progress Report of the Royal Commission on the Aborigines*, vii.
53 C.D. Rowley, *Outcasts in White Australia: Aboriginal Policy and Practice – Volume II* (Canberra: Australian National University Press, 1971), 19.
54 SAPP, *Progress Report of the Royal Commission on the Aborigines*, ix.
55 SAPP, *Final Report of the Royal Commission on The Aborigines*, no. 21 (Adelaide: Government Printer, 1916), iii, iv, vi.
56 Raynes, *'A Little Flour and a Few Blankets',* 39. Note that Koonibba continued to be run by the Lutheran Church until 1961: Mattingley and Hampton, *Survival in Our Own Land*, 209.
57 *Advertiser,* 14 November 1912, 11.
58 SAPP, *Progress Report of the Royal Commission on the Aborigines*, 120.

Chapter 5 ~ South Australia's British farm apprenticeship scheme

1 Including revisiting relevant aspects of Elspeth Grant and Paul Sendziuk, '"Urban Degeneration and Rural Revitalisation": The South Australian Government's youth migration scheme, 1913–14', *Australian Historical Studies* 41, no. 1 (2010): 75–89.
2 With Frederick Young, Commissioner for Crown Lands and Immigration (centre right), Edgar Field, Immigration Officer (centre left), and David Davidson, Assistant Immigration Officer (centre middle): History SA, South Australian Government Photographic Collection, GN01102.
3 John Cashen, 'Social Foundations of South Australia: "Owners of Labour"', in *The Flinders History of South Australia*, ed. Eric Richards (Adelaide: Wakefield Press, 1986), 105–114; *Immigration Act 1872, Immigration Act 1911, Immigration Act Amendment Act 1913;* Michael Williams, *The Making of the South Australian Landscape* (London: Academic Press, 1974), 39–45.
4 Kevin Rudd, Australian Prime Minister, 'Transcript of address at the apology to the Forgotten Australians and former child migrants', 16 November 2009, accessed 14 July 2015, http://pandora.nla.gov.au/pan/110625/20091116-1801/www.pm.gov.au/node/6321.html, and Gordon Brown, British Prime Minister, 'Prime Minister's statement: Child migration', 25 February 2010, accessed 14 July 2015, http://www.parliament.uk/business/news/2010/02/prime-ministers-statement-child-migration/.

5 Geoffrey Sherington, *Australia's Immigrants 1788–1978* (North Sydney: Allen and Unwin, 1980), 94–95, and his body of research on child and youth migration thereafter.

6 Eric Richards, *Destination Australia* (Sydney: UNSW Press, 2008), 64. See also Michele Langfield, *More People Imperative: Immigration to Australia, 1901–39* (Canberra: National Archives of Australia, 1999), 14.

7 Women and girls were usually provided assisted passages for employment in domestic service in both the city and country, as was the case in South Australia; see Margrette Kleinig, 'Independent women: South Australia's assisted immigrants, 1872–1939', in *Visible Women: Female immigrants in colonial Australia*, ed. Eric Richards (Canberra: Australian National University, 1995), 113.

8 Grant and Sendziuk, '"Urban degeneration and rural revitalisation"', 75–89, and Daniel Gorman, *Imperial Citizenship: Empire and the question of belonging* (Manchester: Manchester University Press, 2006), 178–204. Gorman erroneously concludes that Sedgwick's 'experiment' was limited to New Zealand and Canada in 1911–1913, as he does not address Sedgwick's initiation of the British farm apprenticeship scheme in South Australia (spanning 1913–1929), nor Sedgwick's ongoing involvement in youth migration after the First World War (until his death in 1929). This may be because Gorman's main primary sources were Sedgwick's scrapbooks, from which his South Australian exploits are omitted; South Australia's British farm apprentices may have been the subject of the missing third album: Albums 1, 2 and 4, 1910–1914, GBR/0115/RCMS31, Library of the Royal Commonwealth Society, Cambridge University, Cambridge.

9 It is likely that the government also sought to avoid further investment in training farms following its unsuccessful venture at North Booborowie. Such farm schools were not in the same league as the Roseworthy Agricultural College (established in 1883), and in 1913 Peter Waite had only just declared his intent to bequeath what was to become the University of Adelaide's Waite Agricultural Research Institute, South Australia's other leading agricultural education institution.

10 Richards, *Destination Australia*, 40.

11 Richards, *Destination Australia*, 55, and Geoffrey Sherington, 'Contrasting narratives in the history of twentieth-century British child migration to Australia', *History Australia* 9, no. 2 (2012): 27–47.

12 Richards, *Destination Australia*, 28–57, and Williams, *Making of the South Australian Landscape*, 50–55.

13 'Agricultural Bureau Congress 1913', *Department of Agriculture Bulletin* 81 (1913): 6.

14 South Australian Government, 'Opportunity for boys to become farmers' (Adelaide: Government Printers, 1914).

15 *Journal of the Department of Agriculture of South Australia* 17, no. 3 (1913): 409.

16 John Hirst, *Adelaide and the Country, 1870–1917: Their social and political relationship* (Melbourne: Melbourne University Press, 1973), 3; Michelle

Hetherington, introduction to *Glorious Days: Australia 1913*, ed. Michelle Hetherington (Canberra: National Museum of Australia Press, 2013), xi.

17 Grant and Sendziuk, '"Urban degeneration and rural revitalisation"', 75–89, and Richards, *Destination Australia*, 48.

18 *Journal of the Department of Agriculture of South Australia,* 15, no. 2 (1911): 130–132.

19 *Journal of the Department of Agriculture of South Australia,* 15, no. 9 (1912): 976–977.

20 *Journal of the Department of Agriculture of South Australia*, 15, no. 12 (1912): 1304.

21 'Boys for Booborowie training farm', *Register,* 27 March 1912, 10, and 'The Booborowie farm', *Burra Record*, 31 July 1912, 3.

22 *Journal of the Department of Agriculture of South Australia*, 16, no. 3 (1912): 260–261.

23 *Journal of the Department of Agriculture of South Australia*, 17, no. 3 (1912): 409.

24 Files 53, 99–106, 135–138 and 156–164, 'Applications for assisted passage by agricultural labourers', 1911–1914, series GRG7/3, State Records of South Australia (SRSA), Adelaide.

25 *South Australian Parliamentary Debates, House of Assembly*, 30 October 1913, 754.

26 *Journal of the Department of Agriculture of South Australia*, 16, no. 12 (1913): 1432, emphasis added.

27 'Applications for assisted passage by agricultural labourers'.

28 Files 18, 55, 103, 119, 169, 'Applications for assisted passage by agricultural labourers'.

29 'Applications for assisted passage by agricultural labourers', *Journal of the Department of Agriculture of South Australia,* 1911–1914.

30 File 144, 'Applications for assisted passage by agricultural labourers'.

31 'Opportunity for boys to become farmers', 1, and 'Agricultural Bureau Congress 1912', *Department of Agriculture Bulletin* 76 (1912): 30.

32 Some boys still made their way onto pastoral properties under their own steam; for example, see file 169, 'Applications for assisted passage by agricultural labourers'.

33 'Opportunity for boys to become farmers', 7, 9.

34 'Opportunity for boys to become farmers', 9.

35 'Opportunity for boys to become farmers', 3, 5–6, 8, 16. It also points out that apprentices may earn double rates of pay during the harvesting period.

36 'Opportunity for boys to become farmers', 6, 8.

37 'Opportunity for boys to become farmers', 12, and 'Applications for assisted passage by agricultural labourers'.

38 'Opportunity for boys to become farmers', 11, 13.

39 'Opportunity for boys to become farmers', 5, and History SA, South Australian Government Photographic Collection, GN11487.

40 'Boys for farmers', *Register*, 16 January 1914, 9, and 'Boy immigrants', *Chronicle*, 24 January 1914, 44.

41 'Applications for assisted passage by agricultural labourers'.

42 John Glen's host reported that the apprentice could 'neither read, write nor count' but Glen still sent letters, apparently dictated: file 135, 'Applications for assisted passage by agricultural labourers'. Others may have concealed their illiteracy by not writing at all but most files contain at least one letter.

43 Senate Community Affairs References Committee, *Lost Innocents: Righting the record* (Canberra: Commonwealth of Australia, 2001), 137–176.

44 File 37, 'Applications for assisted passage by agricultural labourers'.

45 'Applications for assisted passage by agricultural labourers'.

46 See also the smaller archive 'Applications to Crown Lands Office by South Australian residents for agricultural labourers', 1912–1914, series GRG7/4, SRSA, Adelaide.

47 Rebecca Jones, '1914: A monument to drought', accessed 14 July 2015, http://history.cass.anu.edu.au/monthinhistory/1914-monument-drought. Jones is a Postdoctoral Fellow researching 'Slow Catastrophes: Drought resilience amongst farmers and agricultural communities in Australia, 1880s–2000s', funded by an ARC Discovery Early Career Research Award.

48 For example, Williams, *Making of the South Australian Landscape*, figure 74, and Trevor Griffin and Murray McCaskill, eds, *Atlas of South Australia* (Adelaide: South Australian Government, 1986), 51.

49 File 145, 'Applications for assisted passage by agricultural labourers'.

50 File 29, 'Applications for assisted passage by agricultural labourers'.

51 File 173, 'Applications for assisted passage by agricultural labourers'.

52 File 185, 'Applications for assisted passage by agricultural labourers'.

53 'Applications for assisted passage by agricultural labourers'.

54 File 26, 'Applications for assisted passage by agricultural labourers'.

55 File 181, 'Applications for assisted passage by agricultural labourers'.

56 File 148, 'Applications for assisted passage by agricultural labourers'.

57 Files 137 and 163, 'Applications for assisted passage by agricultural labourers'.

58 File 148, 'Applications for assisted passage by agricultural labourers'.

59 'Applications for assisted passage by agricultural labourers'.

60 Apart from two shillings and sixpence pocket money per week, the government saved the apprentices' wages on their behalf and an apprentice could not access these funds until he turned 21: 'Opportunity for boys to become farmers', 5.

61 File 148, 'Applications for assisted passage by agricultural labourers'.

62 File 146, 'Applications for assisted passage by agricultural labourers'.

63 Williams, *Making of the South Australian Landscape*, 55.

64 'Opportunity for boys to become farmers', 9.
65 File 156, 'Applications for assisted passage by agricultural labourers'.
66 Applications for assisted passage by agricultural labourers' Note also that Simpson did not enlist until after the drought was over: Alexander Galbraith Simpson, regimental no. 2788, 1914–1920, 'First Australian Imperial Force personnel dossiers', Base Records Office, Australian Imperial Force, B2455, National Archives of Australia, Canberra.
67 File 138, 'Applications for assisted passage by agricultural labourers'.
68 'Applications for assisted passage by agricultural labourers'.
69 'Applications for assisted passage by agricultural labourers'.
70 File 137, 'Applications for assisted passage by agricultural labourers'.
71 'Applications for assisted passage by agricultural labourers'.
72 File 166, 'Applications for assisted passage by agricultural labourers'.
73 'Applications for assisted passage by agricultural labourers'; Richards, *Destination Australia*, 64.
74 For example, when Wray wrote 'I supposed there is no chance of sending [Bickerstaff] back to Scotland, as I was told tonight he would like to go back': File 138, 'Applications for assisted passage by agricultural labourers'.
75 File 37, 'Applications for assisted passage by agricultural labourers'.
76 File 148, 'Applications for assisted passage by agricultural labourers'. *Journal of the Department of Agriculture of South Australia* 17.3 (1913): 409.
77 Richards, *Destination Australia*, 64–66.
78 Presumably not realising that they would be repatriated to South Australia at the war's end: Elspeth Grant, 'Homeward bound?', *Wartime* 42 (2008): 35–37.
79 Supporting Michael McKernan's observations regarding 'a different impact the war may have had on city and country': *The Australian People and the Great War* (West Melbourne: Thomas Nelson, 1980), 178–200.
80 Namely Charles Frederick John Akehurst, Cecil Raymond Abbey Brangwin, Archibald Menzies Cameron, William George Chasteauneuf, Andrew Brand Curd, Arthur Floate, John Forrest, Richard Leander Gay, Ernest Albert Green, William Hamilton, Eric James Jarrett, Arthur Percy Martin, Albert Charles Rogers, John Scott, Laurence Semple, Alexander Galbraith Simpson, Percy William Verrell and Walter Wainwright.
81 'Collision on the East-West Railway', *Transcontinental*, 15 May 1915, 2; 'East-West Railway Collision', *Transcontinental*, 12 June 1915, 5; and file 31, 'Applications for assisted passage by agricultural labourers'.
82 Williams, *Making of the South Australian Landscape*, 55.
83 File 179, 'Applications for assisted passage by agricultural labourers'.
84 'Applications for assisted passage by agricultural labourers'.
85 File 193, 'Applications for assisted passage by agricultural labourers'; Jarrett family member, Nigel McLeod, personal communication, 2010.

86 Williams, *Making of the South Australian Landscape*, 297, and Elspeth Grant, 'The Barwell Boys: Centenary of SA's British farm apprentices' (Adelaide: Barwell Boys and Little Brothers Family and Friends Association, 2013).

Chapter 6 ~ Eyre Peninsula on the eve of the Great War

1 According to the Official Year Book of the Commonwealth in 1914, 'the [SA] aboriginal natives enumerated at the census of 1911' totalled 802 males, 637 females and 692 'half castes'.
2 C.E.W. Bean, *On the Wool Track* (Sydney: Angus & Robertson, Sirius Books, 1963), 32.
3 *Chronicle*, 3 January 1914, 35.
4 See, for example, *Chronicle*, 4 July 1914, 36, which carried eight small articles about different aspects of the Sarajevo assassinations. The issue of 1 August included the editorial, war-related 'Cable News' and a map of 'The Probable Theatre of War', 34–35, 37 and 45; on 8 August the issue included maps detailing the British and German navies, editorial, cable news, photos of all belligerent rulers, war news, plus local and national Australian responses, 30, 34–37, 41–47.
5 *Chronicle*, 28 March 1914, 35.
6 *Chronicle*, 16 May 1914, 38.
7 See *Chronicle*, 21 February 1914, 21, for a report of Australia's naval fleet visiting SA, and in an interview with the Admiral, Boston Bay's suitability being explored.
8 *Report of the [SA] Royal Commission on Wharves and Water Frontage, 1911*, 188–194.
9 Jill Roe, 'Voluntary action and the rural poor in the age of globalization', in *Beveridge and Voluntary Action in Britain and the wider British World*, Melanie Oppenheimer and Nicolas Deakin, eds, (Manchester: Manchester University Press, 2011), 109–120.
10 *West Coast Sentinel*, 21 August 1914, 5.
11 *Chronicle*, 17 January 1914, 35.
12 See *Eyre's Peninsula Tribune* of 10, 17 and 24 April 1914, 2.
13 *Chronicle*, 31 January 1914, 12; P.A. Howell, 'Bosanquet, Sir Day Hort (1843–1923)', ADB, ACB, ANU, published first in hardcopy 1979, accessed 13 October 2016, http://adb.anu.edu.au/biography/bosanquet-sir-day-hort-5298/text8941.
14 *Chronicle*, 25 April 1914, 44; P.A. Howell, 'Galway, Sir Henry Lionel (1859–1949)', ADB, ACB, ANU, published first in hardcopy 1981, accessed 13 October 2016 http://adb.anu.edu.au/biography/galway-sir-henry-lionel-6371/text10805.
15 *Chronicle*, 7 March 1914, 45.
16 *Chronicle*, 4 July 1914, 34.
17 *Sentinel*, 14 August 1914, 2.
18 One element of Kitchener's military scheme incorporated into the 1910 Defence Act involved compulsory military training for boys aged

between 12 and 18 years. Opposition was widespread, with parents prosecuted for non-compliance from March 1912. But in South Australia at Easter 1912, three Quakers formed the Australian Freedom League in Gawler. This was followed by meetings in Adelaide and interstate during April and May 1912; see Thomas W. Tanner, *Compulsory Soldiers* (Sydney: Alternative Publishing Cooperative Limited, 1980), 193–199.

19 'Cowell', *Explore Australia*, 2010, accessed 15 May 2016, http://www.exploreaustralia.net.au/South-Australia/Eyre-Peninsula-and-Nullarbor/Cowell.

20 *The Personal Touch. A look at South Australia's postal history* (Adelaide: Australia Post, 1986), 8, 15.

21 Jill Roe, *Our Fathers Clear the Bush: Remembering Eyre Peninsula,* Adelaide: Wakefield Press, 2016), 105–106.

22 See Christobel Mattingley and Ken Hampton, eds, *Survival in Our Own Land: Aboriginal Experiences in 'South Australia' since 1836* (Victoria: Australian Scholarly Publishing, 1988), 202–209, for discussion of Koonibba Mission.

23 The Royal Commission on South Australia's Aborigines was appointed on 19 December 1912, producing an interim report in October 1913 and its final report in 1916.

24 *Sentinel*, 28 August 1914, 5.

25 Peggy Brock, *Outback ghettos: Aborigines, institutionalisation and survival* (Melbourne: Cambridge University Press, 1983); Kay Whitehead and Ben Wadham, 'Marking a Marginal Past: Schooling and dispossession in the Franklin Harbour district', *History Australia* 8, no. 3 (2011): 39–40.

26 Neil and Val Thompson, eds, *The Streaky Bay: a history of the Streaky Bay District Council area* (Compiled by the History Committee of Streaky Bay and District area), (Streaky Bay: Streaky Bay District Council, 1988), 132.

27 Thompson and Thompson, *The Streaky Bay*, 133.

28 *West Coast Recorder*, 20 March 1914, 2.

29 *Sentinel*, 21 August 1914, 5.

30 *West Coast Recorder*, August 1914, 2.

31 Carl Bridge, *A Trunk Full of Books. History of the State Library and its Forerunners*, (Adelaide: Wakefield Press, 1986); Carl Bridge and Michael Talbot, 'Public Libraries', in *The Wakefield Companion to South Australian History*, ed. Wilfrid Prest, Kerrie Round and Carol Fort (Adelaide: Wakefield Press, 2001), 431–433.

32 See *West Coast Recorder*, 30 September, 2, and 14 October 1914, 2.

33 *West Coast Recorder*, 5 August 1914, 2.

34 See *West Coast Recorder*, 16 September, 2, for description of the Tumby Bay 'plain and fancy dress ball', at which 40 'Lincolnites were noticed', and issue of 25 November 1914, 5, for account of a 'successful patriotic concert' held at North Shields, 10 kilometres from Port Lincoln. Two pianists, eight singers and the local school children were mentioned, with 40 or 50 present.

Chapter 7 ~ Town planning in the 'Garden City of the South'

1 Robert Freestone, *Urban Nation: Australia's Planning Heritage* (Canberra: CSIRO Publishing, 2010), 16.

2 Christine Garnaut, 'Towards metropolitan organisation: Town planning and the garden city idea' in *The Australian metropolis: A planning history*, Stephen Hamnett and Robert Freestone, eds (Sydney: Allen & Unwin, 2000), 46.

3 Douglas Pike, *Paradise of Dissent: South Australia 1829–1857* (Carlton: Melbourne University Press, 1967); Robert Home, *Of Planting and Planning: The making of British colonial cities* (London: E & FN Spon, 1997).

4 Pike, *Paradise*, 145–155; Raymond Bunker, 'The Early Years', in *With Conscious Purpose: A History of Town Planning in South Australia*, Alan Hutchings and Raymond Bunker, eds (Adelaide: Wakefield Press, 1986), 8–9.

5 Michael Williams, *The making of the South Australian landscape: A study in the historical geography of Australia* (London: Academic Press, 1974), 24.

6 R.M. Gibbs, *A history of South Australia: From colonial days to the present* (Adelaide: Peacock Publications, 1984), 22; Tony Denholm, 'Adelaide: A Victorian Bastide?', in *The Origins of Australia's Capital Cities*, ed. Pamela Stratham (Cambridge: Cambridge University Press, 1989), 180.

7 Peter Morton, *After Light: A History of the City of Adelaide and its Council, 1878–1928* (Adelaide: Wakefield Press, 1996), 6.

8 Home, *Of Planting*, 9.

9 For discussion of other possible influences, see A. Grenfell Price, *The Foundation and Settlement of South Australia 1829–1845* (1924) (Adelaide: Libraries Board of South Australia, 1973 Facsimile), 109; Williams, *The Making*, 389–397; Bunker, 'The Early Years', 13–15; Donald Leslie Johnson and Donald Langmead, *The Adelaide City Plan: Fiction and Fact* (Adelaide: Wakefield Press, 1986), 9–17; Raymond Bunker, 'Process and product in the foundation and laying out of Adelaide', *Planning Perspectives* 13 (1998): 247–249.

10 Home, *Of Planting* 8; Helen Proudfoot, 'Founding cities in nineteenth-century Australia' in Hamnett and Freestone, *The Australian Metropolis*, 6.

11 Bunker, 'Process and Product', 15–16.

12 Williams, *The Making*, 389.

13 Analysis of the plan based on 'Plan of the City of Adelaide in South Australia' (1837) in *2nd Report of Colonization of South Australia*, London, 1837; Price, *Foundation*, 106–108, 111; Bunker, 'The Early Years', 17; Bunker, 'Process and Product', 251; Johnson and Langmead, *Adelaide City Plan*, 27–29.

14 Price, *Foundation*, 105.

15 Price, *Foundation*, 111. For date see Susan Marsden, Paul Stark and Patricia Sumerling, eds, *Heritage of the City of Adelaide: An Illustrated Guide* (Adelaide: Corporation of the City of Adelaide, 1990), 18.
16 *Register*, 17 February 1838, 14 July 1838, quoted in Price, *Foundation*, 111–112.
17 Bridget Jolly, *Historic South West Corner* (Adelaide: Corporation of the City of Adelaide, 2003), 4, 18.
18 Donald Langmead, *Accidental Architect: The Life and Times of George Strickland Kingston* (Sydney: Crossing Press, 1994), 118, 126, 180.
19 By the end of 1838 town acres were selling for £2000. Price, *Foundation*, 114.
20 Patricia Sumerling, 'Adelaide's West End', in *William Shakespeare's Adelaide 1860–1930*, ed. Brian Dickey (Adelaide: Association of Professional Historians, 1992), 28.
21 J.F. Bennett quoted in Williams, *The Making*, 15.
22 Williams, *The Making*, 413.
23 Bunker, 'The Early Years', 17.
24 Marsden et al., *Heritage*, 21.
25 Rhonda Harris, 'The "Aboriginal Location" in the Adelaide Parklands (1837–1851)' in *Proceedings The Adelaide Parklands Symposium*, Christine Garnaut and Kerrie Round, eds (Adelaide: Centre for Settlement Studies and Bob Hawke Prime Ministerial Centre, 2006), 56–72.
26 Elizabeth Kwan, *Living in South Australia: A Social History* (Adelaide: South Australian Government Printer, 1987), 56; Morton, *After Light*, 16.
27 Emily Clark in Kwan, *Living*, 56.
28 Charles Barton in Kwan, *Living*, 56.
29 Alison Painter, 'Hotels and Drinking', in *William Shakespeare's Adelaide*, 87.
30 Discussion of villages based on Price, *Foundation*, 174–175, and Williams, *The Making*, 400–403.
31 Thomas Worsnop, *History of the City of Adelaide from the foundation of the province of South Australia in 1836 to the end of the municipal year 1877* (Adelaide: J. Williams, 1878).
32 Williams, *The Making*, 421–423.
33 Denholm, 'Adelaide', 185.
34 Denholm, 'Adelaide', 183.
35 Julie Collins, 'Adelaide's Early Skyline', *Place* 44 (2014): 22–23.
36 R.M. Gibbs, *Under the Burning Sun: A history of colonial South Australia 1836–1900* (Adelaide: Southern Heritage, 2013), 286–329.
37 Morton, *After Light*, xiii.
38 Williams, *The Making*, 42.
39 See maps by Ann Marshall in 'The development of Adelaide 1837–1963', *Building Ideas* 2, no. 4 (1963): 3–25, and reproduced in Williams, *The Making*, 418.

40 Based on Morton, *After Light*, xi–xiii and 180–185 unless otherwise noted.
41 Peter Donovan and Alison Painter, *Real History: The Real Estate Institute of South Australia, 1919–1989* (Adelaide: Real Estate Institute of South Australia, 1989), 47; Williams, *The Making*, 433.
42 Donovan and Painter, *Real History*, 49.
43 Walter Creese, *The Search for Environment: The garden city before and after* (New Haven: Yale University Press, 1966).
44 Peter Hall, *Cities of tomorrow: An intellectual history of urban planning and design since 1880* (Chichester: Wiley Blackwell, 2014); Stephen V. Ward, *Planning the Twentieth Century City: The advanced capitalist world* (Chichester: John Wiley & Sons, 2002).
45 Ward, *Planning*, 12–16.
46 J.A. Peterson, *The Birth of City Planning in the United States, 1840–1917* (Baltimore: Johns Hopkins University, 2003).
47 Peter Hall and Colin Ward, *Sociable Cities: the legacy of Ebenezer Howard* (Chichester: John Wiley & Sons, 1998).
48 Alan Hutchings, 'From theory to practice: The inter-war years' in Hamnett and Freestone, *The Australian Metropolis*, 65.
49 Morton, *After Light*, xii.
50 J.B Hirst, *Adelaide and the Country 1870–1917: Their social and political relationship* (Carlton: Melbourne University Press, 1973), 60.
51 M. Twain, *More Tramps Abroad* (1897) quoted in Corporation of the City of Adelaide, *Official Illustrated Guide* (Adelaide: Corporation of the City of Adelaide, n.d.), 42.
52 Christine Garnaut, *Colonel Light Gardens: model garden suburb*, (Sydney: Crossing Press, 2006), 17–19; Christine Garnaut and Kerrie Round, '"Pedlers of new ideas": Promoting town planning in South Australia 1914–1924' in *Cities, Citizens and Environmental Reform: Histories of Australian Town Planning* Associations, ed. Robert Freestone (Sydney: Sydney University Press, 2009), 120.
53 Corporation, *Official Illustrated Guide*, 42.
54 Draft of a circular re town planning to the Commissioner of Crown Lands, 1913, GRG 35/1/1913/157, State Records of South Australia (SRSA), Adelaide.
55 *Register*, 19 July 1913; GRG 35/1/1913/157, SRSA, Adelaide.
56 Corporation of the City of Adelaide, *Annual Report* 1912, 67.
57 Robert Freestone, 'An Imperial Aspect: The Australasian Town Planning Tour of 1914–15', *Australian Journal of Politics and History*, 44, no. 2 (1998), 159–176.
58 Corporation of the City of Adelaide, *Annual Report* 1911, 47.

Chapter 8 ~ Indians contesting White Australia

1 Marilyn Lake, 'On Being a White Man Australia, circa 1900' in *Cultural History in Australia*, Hsu-Ming Teo and Richard White, eds (Sydney: University of NSW Press, 2003), 98.

2 A. Palfreeman, *The Administration of the White Australia Policy* (Melbourne: Melbourne University Press, 1967), 146; A.T. Yarwood, *Asian Migration to Australia* (Melbourne: Melbourne University Press,1967), 163.

3 Elizabeth Kwan, 'Parsons, John Langdon (1837–1903)', ADB, ACB, ANU, published first in hardcopy 1988, accessed 18 February 2016, http://adb.anu.edu.au/biography/parsons-john-langdon-7966/text13871.

4 John Playford, 'Kingston, Charles Cameron (1850–1908)', ADB, NCB, ANU, published first in hardcopy 1983, accessed 18 February 2016, http://adb.anu.edu.au/biography/kingston-charles-cameron-6966/text12099. See also *The Herald*, the newspaper of the labour movement in South Australia, 28 September 1901, 5–6.

5 *Advertiser*, 2 October 1900, 5.

6 Hugh Tinker, *A New System of Slavery: The Export of Indian Labour Overseas 1820–1920*, (London: Oxford University Press, 1974).

7 *South Australia Register*, 5 October 1900, 7.

8 *Herald*, 26 April 1902, 4.

9 No. 3 1857. An Act to make provision for levying a charge on Chinese arriving in South Australia; No. 14 1861. An Act to repeal an Act No. 3 of 1857–1858, entitled 'An Act to make provision for levying a charge on Chinese arriving in South Australia'; No. 213 1881. The Chinese Immigrants Regulation Act; No. 439 1888. Chinese Immigration Restriction Act; No. 474 1889. An Act to amend the 'Chinese Immigration Restriction Act, 1888'; No. 494 1890. An Act to further amend the 'Chinese Immigration Restriction Act, 1888'; No. 534 1891. An Act to continue the 'Chinese Immigration Restriction Act, 1888.' This list at State Library of South Australia (SLSA), *Multicultural Heritage; Chinese in Australia 1950s–1914*, accessed 4 February 2016, http://guides.slsa.sa.gov.au/content.php?pid=126605&sid=1086762.

10 For a similar outcry in Victoria, see Nadia Rhook, '"Turban-clad" British Subjects Tracking the Circuits of Mobility, Visibility, and Sexuality in Settler Nation-Making', *Transfers* 3, no. 3 (2015):104–122.

11 See reports in *Register* 22 April, 1 May, 5 July and 7 July 1893.

12 *Register*, 5 July 1893, 4.

13 *Advertiser*, 13 December 1899, 5. The term 'Hindoo' was used to refer to people from India, whether they were Sikhs, Muslims or Hindus.

14 Letter to *Register*, 1 December 1905. See another supportive letter from Dumosa in *Register*, 7 December 1905.

15 Gordon Lillias, 'The Orient League: Its Relation to our Politics', *Critic* (Adelaide), 18 August 1909, 5.

16 Lillias, 'The Orient League', 5.

17 *Advertiser*, 22 September 1899, 4.
18 Margaret Allen, 'Shadow letters and the Karnana letter: Indians negotiate the White Australia Policy, 1901–1921', *Life Writing*, no. 2 (2011): 187–202.
19 National Archives, Kew, United Kingdom Colonial Office 886/1/3, Correspondence 1897–1908 relating to the treatment of Asiatics in the Dominions. Enclosure 1 in 189, Petition from Western Australia traders of Asiatic origin to Secretary of State for the Colonies.
20 Bhagat Singh, 'The Licensed Hawkers' Bill', *Advertiser*, 7 November 1904, 8.
21 Singh, 'The Licensed Hawkers' Bill', 8.
22 'United Asiatic League', *Register*, 27 September 1905, 4.
23 *Register*, 12 October 1905, 4.
24 *Register*, 12 October 1905, 4.
25 Eric Richards, 'Cohen, Sir Lewis (1849–1933)', ADB, ANC, ANU, published first in hardcopy 1981, accessed 12 February 2016, http://adb.anu.edu.au/biography/cohen-sir-lewis-5716/text9667.
26 *Advertiser*, 23 November 1905, 4.
27 Richards, 'Cohen'.
28 *Advertiser*, 23 November 1905, 4. It is interesting to note that a public meeting about attacks upon Russian Jews at the time of the 1905 Russian revolution was held on the same afternoon. See *Advertiser*, 24 November 1905, 7.
29 Obituary Mr George Gee Wah, *Advertiser*, 17 August 1939, 12.
30 Lillias, 'The Orient League', 11 August 1909, 4.
31 'Patriotic Citizen: The late Mr J.R. Coory', *Daily Herald*, 28 September 1912, 7.
32 'The outcry against Asiatics', *Register* 11 July 1893, 5.
33 'Asiatics', *Register*, 14 July 1893, 5. Swift seems to have taken up a number of points made by W. Haslam MLC in the Legislative Council on 11 July. See the Coory brothers' response: 'The Hon. W. Haslam and Asiatics', *Advertiser*, 31 July 1893.
34 'Messrs. Coory brothers and Asiatics', *Register*, 22 July 1893, 6.
35 *Register*, 19 November 1906, 5; *Advertiser*, 19 November 1906, 6.
36 *Advertiser*, 19 November 1906, 6.
37 *Register*, 3 December 1908, 3.
38 *Advertiser*, 3 December 1908, 3.
39 *Register*, 22 December 1909, 4.
40 *Sport* (Adelaide), 20 January 1912, 8.
41 Gordon, 'The Orient League' 5.
42 Gordon, 'The Orient League' 5.
43 Gordon, 'The Orient League' 5.
44 National Archives of Australia: B2455, SINGH SARN.

Chapter 9 ~ German South Australia on the eve of war

1 On the history of the 'German concentration camp' on Torrens Island see especially Peter Monteath, Mandy Paul and Rebecca Martin, *Interned: Torrens Island 1914–1915* (Adelaide: Wakefield Press, 2014).

2 Ian Harmstorf and Michael Cigler, *The Germans in Australia* (Melbourne: AE Press, 1985), 12–14.

3 The idea of South Australia as a 'paradise of dissent' is most closely associated with the historian Douglas Pike and his book *Paradise of Dissent: South Australia, 1829–1857* (Melbourne: Melbourne University Press, 1967).

4 There are many examples of such guides 'spruiking' the benefits of immigration to South Australia. For a concise overview see '"*Dieses schöne Land*": Spruiking South Australia 1848/1849', in Herbert Stock (ed.), *Becoming South Australian: Germans in a British context* (Adelaide: n.p., 201), 3–10. For the exceptional, critical account see Gustav Listemann, *Meine Auswanderung nach Süd-Australien und Rückkehr zum Vaterlande. Ein Wort zur Warnung und Belehrung für alle Auswanderungslustigen* (Berlin: A.W. Hayn, 1851).

5 Friedrich Gerstaecker, *Narrative of a Journey Round the World* (New York: Harper & Brothers, 1853), 462.

6 Josef Vondra, *German Speaking Settlers in Australia* (Melbourne: Cavalier Press, 1981), 55.

7 Jürgen Tampke, *The Germans in Australia* (Cambridge: Cambridge University Press, 2006), 31–32.

8 *Australische Zeitung*, 22 September 1897. A helpful analysis of how the Adelaide press dealt with the issue of German loyalty is in Ian Harmstorf, '1838–1890: The Issue of Loyalty – South Australian Germans', *The German Club*, accessed 15 August 2015, http://www.thegermanclub.com.au/about-us/german-history-in-SA.php#Year1838to1990.

9 *Adelaide Observer*, 18 April 1857.

10 *Adelaide Times*, 8 June 1857.

11 Ian Harmstorf, 'Guests or Fellow-Countrymen. A Study of Assimilation: An Aspect of the German Community in South Australia 1836–1918'(PhD thesis, Flinders University, 1987), 42.

12 Harmstorf, 'Guests or Fellow-Countrymen', 35.

13 Harmstorf, '1838–1890: The Issue of Loyalty'.

14 Harmstorf, 'Guests or Fellow-Countrymen', 104.

15 Matthew 22: 21. In the case of Luther's theology, the relevant point here is his '*Zwei-Reiche-Lehre*', that is, the doctrine of the two kingdoms. In this thinking, the kingdom of God is considered to be separate from the earthly or secular realm and should remain so.

16 *Southern Australian*, 1 May 1839.

17 South Australian Archives, PRG 174/1/1390—1393, Cited in Ian Harmstorf, '1838–1890: The Issue of Loyalty'.

18 *Australische Zeitung*, 24 June 1896.

19 Philip Jones, 'Colonial *Wissenschaft*: German Naturalists and Museums in Nineteenth-Century South Australia', in *Germans: Travellers, Settlers and Their Descendants in South Australia*, ed. Peter Monteath (Adelaide, Wakefield Press, 2011), 226.
20 *Australische Zeitung*, 29 November 1899.
21 On the history and practice of *Deutschtumspolitik* in Australia, see especially John A. Moses, '"*Deutschtumspolitik*" in Australia from Kaiserreich to Third Reich. Problems of Promoting Germany in Australia from Hirschfeld to von Luckner', in *The German Experience of Australia 1833–1938*, Ian Harmstorf and Peter Schwertfeger, eds (Adelaide: The Australian Association of Humboldt Fellows, 1988), 120–136; see also Irmline Veit-Brause, 'Australia as an "Object" in Nineteenth Century World Affairs: The Example of the German Consular Representations in the Australian Colonies', *Australian Journal of Politics and History* 34, no. 2 (1988): 142–159.
22 Cited in Johannes Voigt, 'The German National Festival in Sydney before World War I', in *New Beginnings: The Germans in New South Wales and Queensland*, ed. Johannes Voigt (Stuttgart: Institut für Auslandsbeziehungen, 1983), 144.
23 Harmstorf, 'Guests or Fellow-Countrymen', 23.
24 Harmstorf, 'Guests or Fellow-Countrymen', 81.
25 Tampke, *The Germans in Australia*, 112.
26 Theodor Hebart, *Die Vereinigte Evangelische Lutheranische Kirche in Australien* (Adelaide: Lutheran Book Depot, 1938), 469.
27 Kiliani to Reich Chancellor, 1 February 1913, 4, in *German Foreign Affairs Documents*, Australian Joint Copying Project, L266610 28 (Reel 274).
28 Kiliani to Reich Chancellor, 11.
29 Kiliani to Reich Chancellor, 13.
30 Kiliani to Reich Chancellor, 1 February 1913, 14, 16.
31 Kiliani to Reich Chancellor, 9 April 1913, 2, 3, in *German Foreign Affairs Documents*, L266646 47, 2, 3.
32 *Register*, 21 September 1912, 15.
33 Harmstorf, 'Guests or Fellow-Countrymen', 114.
34 Joan Hancock and Eric Richards, 'Muecke, Hugo Carl Emil (1842–1929)', ADB, ANC, ANU, published first in hardcopy 1986, accessed 8 August 2015, http://adb.anu.edu.au/biography/muecke-hugo-carl-emil-7674/text13427.
35 *Australische Zeitung*, 1 September 1909.
36 See Harmstorf, 'Guests or Fellow-Countrymen', 121.

Chapter 10 ~ Irish South Australians in 1914

1 See *Southern Cross*, 8, 15 and 22 May 1914, for reports of meetings where the United Irish League (UIL), the Hibernian Australian Catholic Benefit Society (Hibernians) and the Irish National Forresters (INF) met to coordinate the event.

2 *Advertiser, Daily Mail* and *Register* of 2 June 1914.

3 *Register*, 1 June 1914.

4 See *Southern Cross*, 21 December 1900, for F.B. Keogh's summary of what South Australia's Irish had done for Ireland.

5 *Southern Cross*, 8 May 1914.

6 See *Advertiser*, 10 and 22 June 1914, for letters debating whether it was the Union Jack or the British red Ensign; see also Elizabeth Kwan, *Flag and Nation: Australians and their National Flags since 1901* (Sydney: UNSW Press, 2006), 13–23, for discussion of post-Federation confusion and uncertainty over flags.

7 John O'Reily, born in Kilkenny in 1846, was Adelaide's Archbishop from 1895 to 1915; he was followed by Robert William Spence, born in Cork in 1860, Archbishop from 1915 to 1935.

8 See Table 1 for details of all MPs present.

9 *Daily Herald*, 2 June 1914.

10 Following the 1867 death sentence handed down to Fenians for their part in the 'murder' of a gaoler while rescuing Fenian colleagues in Manchester, one yelled 'God Save Ireland' from the dock. Irish journalist A.M. Sullivan set words to an American Civil War tune. Its radical sentiments ensured popularity; it became the unofficial anthem of the Irish.

11 Early significant Irishmen included G.S. Kingston, R. and R.R. Torrens, C. Bagot, C.B. Newenham, W. and T. O'Halloran, E.B. Gleeson and J. Hope. See *Register*, 3 May 1850, for report of Kingston's speech at the first annual dinner of the St Patrick's Society. Kingston continued to be associated with the Irish community, for example presiding at the 1879 St Patrick's Day Grand National Concert; see *Register*, 18 March 1879.

12 Eric Richards, 'The importance of being Irish in Colonial South Australia', in *The Irish Emigrant Experience in Australia*, John O'Brien and Pauric Travers, eds (Dublin: Poolbeg Press, 1991), 63. 'Ireland gave bone and sinew, capital and skills to South Australia ...'; Ann Herraman, '"A Certain Shade of Green': Aspects of Irish Settlement in Nineteenth-century Colonial South Australia' in *Echoes of Irish Australia: Rebellion to Republic*, Jeff Brownrigg, Cheryl Mongan and Richard Reid, eds (Galong: St Clements Retreat and Conference Centre, 2007), 142.

13 See *Register*, 21 March 1840, 20 March 1841, 25 April 1849, 3 May 1850, 18 March 1851, and *Adelaide Times*, 19 March 1856.

14 Douglas Pike, *Paradise of Dissent: South Australia 1829–1857*, (London: Melbourne University Press, 1957), 275–276.

15 Margaret Press, *From Our Broken Toil: South Australian Catholics 1836–1906* (Adelaide: Archdiocese of Adelaide, 1986), 148.

16 Dr W. Ullathorne, *Biography*, quoted in *Southern Cross*, 4 November 1898.

17 *South Australian*, 10 October 1850.

18 Editorial, *Register*, 9 April 1850.

19 See *Register*, 24 September 1852, 1 and 2 April 1854; 15, 16, 17 November 1854; 24, 25, 26, 27 and 29 January 1855; 22 February 1862; 22 December 1875 and 14 May 1880. See also *Adelaide Times*, 12 December 1855.

20 Press, *From our Broken Toil*, 148.

21 Marie Steiner, *Servants Depots in Colonial South Australia* (Adelaide: Wakefield Press, 2009), 20–23.

22 See *Register*, 9 May 1855.

23 Steiner, *Servants Depots*. See also Stephanie James, 'Becoming South Australians? The Impact of the Irish on the County of Stanley, 1841–1871' (MA thesis, Flinders University, 2009), 119–130, for discussion of the Clare depot in the context of both official and broad district cooperation, and the complete absence of community antagonism.

24 See *Register*,1 June 1904, for a letter headed 'An Overflow of Servant Girls', which opened with 'Just 50 years ago this fair land of South Australia had more servant girls on hand than places could be found for'. Its subsequent tone was not complimentary.

25 See *Advertiser*,12 March 1860.

26 Daly was Governor from 4 March 1862 until his death on 19 February 1868.

27 *Register*, 12 February 1863.

28 P.A. Howell, 'More Varieties of Vice-Regal Life', *Journal of the Historical Society of South Australia*, 9 (1981): 1.

29 *Kapunda Herald*, 12 June 1868.

30 See *Register*, 18 March 1862.

31 See *Register*, 18 March 1862.

32 See *Register*, 21 March 1862.

33 See Patrick O'Farrell, *The Irish in Australia*, Third edition (Sydney: New South Wales University Press, 2000), 211, and Malcolm Campbell, *Ireland's New Worlds: Immigrants, Politics and Society in the United* States *and Australia 1815–1922* (Wisconsin: University of Wisconsin Press, 2008), 114.

34 *Register*, 17 March 1868.

35 *Southern Cross and Catholic Herald*, 20 March 1868.

36 For 88 names of local Irishmen gathered by the police, see 'List of Names of Persons who are suspected of having Sympathy with the object of Fenianism and are otherwise disloyally disposed', GRG 5/2/1868/539, State Records of South Australia (SRSA), Adelaide.

37 Susan Woodburn,' The Irish in New South Wales, Victoria and South Australia, 1788–1880' (MA thesis, University of Adelaide, 1974), 317.

38 *Advertiser*, 22 March 1879.
39 Richards, 'The importance of being Irish in Colonial South Australia', 72–73.
40 Fidelma M. Breen, '"Yet we are told that Australians do not sympathise with Ireland": A Study of South Australian support for Irish Home Rule, 1883 to 1912' (MPhil thesis, University of Adelaide, 2013), 46.
41 *Register*, 18 March 1879.
42 *Register*, 19 March 1894.
43 See *Southern Cross*, 31 January, 1896, and 7, 14 and 21 February 1896.
44 *Register*, 17 March 1896.
45 *Register*, 18 March 1896.
46 O'Loghlin's parents had emigrated in 1840. Born in 1852, he worked on his father's farm before employment as a wheat agent in the mid-north and co-purchasing the *Terowie Enterprise* in 1884, prior to election as a Legislative Councillor in 1888. From 1889 to 1896 he edited the *Southern Cross*, the colony's first persisting Catholic newspaper. He was a delegate to Irish-Australian Conventions in 1883 and 1889, holding executive positions in the Irish National Federation (INF) in the 1890s and the UIL from 1900.
47 Breen, 'And yet we are told'.
48 Although all figures are debatable as sources differ, they represent national amounts. Walshe remained in Australia until 1905.
49 See J.M. Stock, 'The 1916 Conscription Referendum: An Analysis of Voting Patterns in the Rural Areas of South Australia' (PhD thesis, Flinders University, 1978), 314; Breen, 'And yet we are told', 170.
50 Breen, 'And yet we are told', 172.
51 Breen, 'And yet we are told', 172–173.
52 *Southern Cross*, 24 March 1905.
53 'The Royal Commission on the Natural Resources, Trade, and Legislation of Certain Portions of his Majesty's Dominions' gathered evidence in all Australian capital cities during May and June of 1913.
54 *Adelaide Chronicle*, 31 January 1914.
55 *Southern Cross*, 3 July 1914.
56 In Melbourne of the 30 politicians present, 23 were federal and seven state and Labor MPs predominated, see *Advocate*, 9 May 1914.
57 Howard Coxon, John Playford and Robert Reid, *Biographical Register of the South Australian Parliament 1857–1957* (Adelaide: Wakefield Press, 1985).
58 Jenny Stock, 'The 1916 Conscription Referendum', 315.
59 *Daily Herald*, 2 June 1914. See also Coxon, *Biographical Register*.
60 Breen, 'And yet we are told', 153, 150.
61 Breen, 'And yet we are told', 150.
62 *Southern Cross*, 27 October 1905.
63 *Southern Cross*, 9 February 1906.

64 Breen, 'And yet we are told', 159.
65 *Southern Cross*, 3 July 1914.
66 *Daily Herald*, 16 June 1914.
67 *Advertiser,* 18 July 1914, shows numbers attending provided in a court case where a loyalist 'lost his head', used indecent language and was fined £2 with 12/- costs.
68 See *Daily Herald*, *Register* and *Advertiser,* 17 July 1914; their reports differed in length, detail and emotion. Reverend Digges La Touche was a professor of literature.
69 *Register,* 25 July 1914.
70 See *Daily Herald*, 25 July 1914.
71 *Register,* 8 October 1914.

Contributors

Margaret Allen is Professor Emerita in Gender Studies, University of Adelaide, and a member of the Fay Gale Centre for Research on Gender. She researches transnational, postcolonial and gendered histories, in particular, on links between India and Australia from c. 1880–1940. She has published on Australian missionaries in India and the experiences of Indian men negotiating the White Australia Policy. Currently she is working on an ARC team project, 'Beyond Empire transnational religious networks & liberal cosmopolitanisms'.

Margaret Anderson researches and writes on women's history, the history and demography of the family and on aspects of public history. She has held senior positions as a public historian in South Australia, Western Australia and Victoria, and is a Fellow of the Federation of Australian Historical Societies.

John Bannon AO was South Australia's longest-serving Labor premier. Following retirement from politics, he completed a PhD at Flinders University. He was an Adjunct Professor of Law at the University of Adelaide and a Visiting Research Fellow at Flinders University, and spoke and published widely on his specialist area, Australian Federation. In 2007 he was made an officer of the Order of Australia for service to politics, history and the community. Wakefield Press published his *Supreme Federalist: The political life of Sir John Downer* in 2009. John Bannon died on 13 December 2015.

Christine Garnaut is Associate Research Professor in Planning and Architectural History and Director of the Architecture Museum in the School of Art, Architecture and Design at the University of South Australia. Her research focuses on the planning and design history of twentieth-century planned environments, particularly in South Australia.

Elspeth Grant is currently coordinator of English, Humanities and Social Sciences at Mark Oliphant College and a committee member for the History Teachers Association of SA. Her previous roles included curator at the Migration Museum, manager of Ayers House Museum and summer research scholar at the Australian War Memorial. She was named South Australia's Emerging Historian of the Year in 2013. Elspeth's great-grandfather Lewis Grant emigrated to SA under the British farm apprenticeship scheme in 1914 and served in the 1st AIF.

Stephanie James has an abiding interest in history, in particular the contribution of the Irish, the largest colonial minority group, to South Australia. This probably stems from her strongly Irish background. Her MA (2009) looked at the early history of the Irish in the Clare Valley while her PhD focused on issues of Irish-Australian loyalty during times of imperial crisis.

Margrette Kleinig works as a Research Assistant in the School of History and International Relations at Flinders University in South Australia. Her research and writing are in Australian and British history, especially in migration history.

Alison Mackinnon AM is Professor Emerita of the University of South Australia and a Fellow of the Academy of the Social Sciences in Australia. She was the Foundation Director of the Hawke Research Institute at the University of South Australia and has written widely on educational and women's history.

Peter Monteath is Professor of History at Flinders University in Adelaide. Among his publications with Wakefield Press are the collection *Germans: Settlers, Travellers and Their Descendants in South Australia* (2011), and the edited translation of Friedrich Gerstäcker's Australian travelogue, which appeared under the title *Australia: A German Traveller in the Age of Gold* (2016).

Melanie Oppenheimer holds the Chair of History and is Dean of the School of History and International Relations at Flinders University in South Australia. Her research interests focus on women, war and volunteering in the twentieth century, and she has a special interest in soldier settlement and Red Cross history.

Mandy Paul is the Director of the Migration Museum. She has postgraduate qualifications in history and museum studies, and her research interests include South Australian migration and Indigenous history and historical practice in the context of museums and native title law. In 2014 Wakefield Press published *Interned: Torrens Island, 1914–1915*, which she co-authored with Peter Monteath and Rebecca Martin.

Jill Roe AO was one of Australia's finest historians, best known for her biography of Miles Franklin. Born on the Eyre Peninsula, she returned to this subject matter in her last publications including *Our Fathers Cleared the Bush. Remembering Eyre Peninsula* (Wakefield Press, 2016). She died on 12 January 2017.

Index

Arthur Blackburn, VC

An Australian hero, his men, and their two world wars

Andrew Faulkner

Gallipoli hero, Victoria Cross recipient, battalion and brigade commander, conqueror of Damascus and defiant antagonist of the Japanese – by any measure Arthur Seaforth Blackburn was one of Australia's most remarkable soldiers. This, the first Blackburn biography, details the famous battles that shaped Australia. It tells Blackburn's story through the eyes of his comrades, including many from his battalion who survived the horrors of the Burma Railway, and includes photographs taken by Blackburn never published before.

> *'Faulkner has closely liaised with Blackburn's family to bring us a story as factual as can possibly be written. Descriptions of battles and battlefields provide riveting, page-turning reading.'*
> – Donald Lawie, *M/C Reviews*

For more information visit www.wakefieldpress.com.au

GERMANS

Travellers, settlers and their descendants in South Australia

Peter Monteath

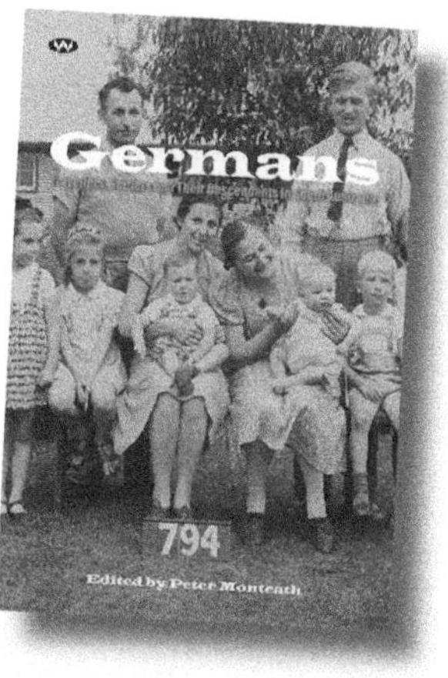

From Beehive Corner and Bert Flugelman's polished balls in Rundle Mall to the vineyards, churches and cemeteries of the Barossa Valley, tangible signs of South Australia's Germans are everywhere to be seen. Too often, however, 'the Germans' are regarded as a single group. The truth is more complex and intriguing.

Those who came during the colony's first decades mostly spoke a common language, but were divided by differences of country, culture and class. They brought an astonishing variety of knowledge and talents, and were destined to make a difference in many fields.

The essays gathered here explore the multiple contributions of Germans in South Australia over some 175 years.

'[A] meticulously researched source for everyone interested in the intricate relationship between Germany and (South) Australia. The clear style and absence of jargon ... render [the book] a worthwhile compendium for scholars and general readers alike.'

– Oliver Haag, *Reviews in Australian Studies*

For more information visit www.wakefieldpress.com.au

Wakefield Press is an independent publishing and distribution company based in Adelaide, South Australia. We love good stories and publish beautiful books. To see our full range of books, please visit our website at www.wakefieldpress.com.au where all titles are available for purchase.

Find us!

Twitter: www.twitter.com/wakefieldpress
Facebook: www.facebook.com/wakefield.press
Instagram: instagram.com/wakefieldpress

www.ingramcontent.com/pod-product-compliance
Ingram Content Group Australia Pty Ltd
76 Discovery Rd, Dandenong South VIC 3175, AU
AUHW011024310725
414624AU00008B/66

9 781743 054741